# Finding the Upside

## Practical Wisdom for Challenging Times

*Here's to Living an Upside Life — Warm Regards, Steve*

STEVE GOLDBERG, ED.M., AND
BARBARA A. TAYLOR, B.A., MMFT

Photo of Steve Goldberg: Olga Dudek ©
Photo of Barbara Taylor: Jeffrey Schmieg ©
Watermark art by Kaley Tallon, 2009 ©
Editorial assistance by Camilla Turner
Cover photo credit: Barbara A. Taylor, 2009
Book design by Jim Bisakowski  BookDesign.ca

ISBN: 978-0-9813434-0-2

10 9 8 7 6 5 4 3 2 1

*To my grandma, dad, and mom — who have each passed on — with gratitude for their unending support and belief in me. Numerous times, they said there was a book in me that needed to be shared with others. I wish they were here to read it.*

STEVE GOLDBERG

*To the mysterious gifts of Soul and to my much-loved family and friends, who continue to help me to learn that what's in the way, is the way.... Thank you.*

BARBARA A. TAYLOR

We are
People who need to love, because
Love is the soul's life,
Love is simply creation's greatest joy.
                    HAFIZ, "The Stairway of Existence"[1]

---

[1] Lines from the poem "The Stairway of Existence," in *The Gift: Poems by Hafiz the Great Sufi Master*, by Daniel Ladinsky (New York: Penguin Group, 1999).

# Contents

## CHAPTER THREE—TAKING STOCK AND CLEARING OUT THE CLUTTER. . . . . . . . . . . . . . . . . . . . . . . . . . . 67

# Introduction

Imagine yourself feeling at peace
with your life as it is.
Not needing to change anything,
yet being open to change
and knowing that change will come.
Trusting your life as a work in progress,
grateful for the hard times and the good times
and all you've learned from your experience.
Doing what you love and loving what you do.
Being curious about your place
in the vast and mysterious web of life.
Cultivating awareness and
allowing your heart to open.
Feeling fully alive:
full of curiosity, wonder, and imagination.
Being comfortable with impermanence,
knowing that—whatever the situation—this too shall pass.
Believing that you are in the right place, at the right time.
Trusting your insides
and your ability to read the signs and signals
that guide your life.
Nurturing your physical body.
Taking time to play and connect with others.

Seeking balance in all your relationships.
Living within your means
and sharing your wealth and experience with others.
Valuing your unique path.

Being you—meeting life in the present moment
and finding the upside in both its gifts and its challenges—
allowing life to unfold and living it to the fullest.
BARBARA A. TAYLOR

I t's a beautiful series of thoughts, isn't it? Feeling at peace with your life as it is, loving what you do, trusting your insides, and knowing that whatever the present circumstances, this too shall pass. For most of us, however, it's hard to read those lines without feeling a little wistful (perhaps after an initial soft sigh of hope) or even downright critical: "Yeah, right. Maybe someday, but certainly not now! Things are a mess these days, and they don't seem to be getting any better. Who has the time or resources for such unrealistic and idealistic notions?"

Do things need to be better—in our work or personal life, in the state of our bank account and the world economy, or in the condition of the planet—in order for us to be okay, right now, today?

Is real change what is observable and measurable in the outside world around us? Or does it have more to do with what we think and how we feel on the inside, which thereby affects our experience of the outside world?

## Steve's story:
## "A silver lining in the doom and gloom"

Who among us hasn't been shaken up to some degree by the current economic and financial upheaval? According to reports, the residual effects of the Great Recession could be with us for a long time to come. The list seems endless: mortgage meltdowns, the housing and credit crisis, bank closings, job cuts and unemployment rates, fluctuating costs for fuel and groceries, losses of savings and investments, and the grim realization that North America's plight pales in comparison with many other locations in the world.

We could easily become gripped with fear, anxiety, and/ or depression over the formidable challenges we're facing in our personal and work lives. But what if Thomas Moore, psychotherapist and author of several books, including *Care of the Soul*,[1] is right? What if our most opportune times to cultivate depth and genuineness in our lives—to grow and develop *soul*—are those times when we are out of balance, shaken out of the comfort of our usual day-to-day patterns and the sleepy complacency they induce? It is during the challenging times that we are brought back to basics, including a fresh and searching look at what really matters to us and what brings meaning to our lives.

In my work as a personal and executive coach, I've been observing a curious thing lately: despite hardship, fear, and worry about the future, a significant number of

---

[1] Thomas Moore's book, Care of the Soul: A guide for cultivating depth and sacredness in everyday life (New York: HarperCollins, 1992), offers a philosophy of soulful living and techniques for dealing with everyday problems without striving for perfection or "salvation."

people report that their lives have actually *improved* as a result of the financial and economic challenges they face.

In my conversations with numerous people, I would at first hear about the difficult and sometimes devastating things that were happening in their lives. But as their discussions deepened and the core elements of the various situations came into view, I would notice that not all of what they were describing seemed *negative* to them. I would then introduce questions to expand on my understanding of their experience: "What else was going on?"; "Were you surprised by your reaction to the situation?"; "Now that you are reflecting on it further, do you think there is an Upside to this whole thing?"; or "Are there any other Upsides that come to mind?"

Many told me that they had been spending more quality time with family and friends rather than their usual modes of entertainment, which were often costly. Others commented on the satisfaction they were getting from reflecting on and shifting some of their core values, their lifestyles and their spending habits. A few described what I would call *resilience*, a growing awareness that they were becoming wiser and more adaptable through the choices they were making to organize key aspects of their lives with new priorities. And many were surprised and humbled when they acted to reach out and help others who were in worse shape, even as their own personal finances were diminishing.

It occurred to me that these individuals were coming to terms with a new sense of what mattered most to them. They were discovering that in humanistic terms, *net worth* had very little to do with *true wealth*. In their own ways, they were finding the Upside in their lives. They were, without exception, excited about and grateful for what they were learning about themselves. They were turning adversity into opportunity.

From these conversations, I distilled five core elements that seemed instrumental in leading to the experience of these Upsides:

■ Cultivating resilience and maintaining optimism

■ Spending less, choosing wisely, and enjoying more

■ Taking stock and clearing out clutter to make room for the things that matter most

■ Paying fresh attention to here-and-now circumstances and beginning to accept and learn from what life is offering, all its gifts and its challenges

■ Discovering authentic giving and making a difference in others' lives

While we can't control what life brings to our door or even the full extent of the consequences of our actions, we are completely free to choose our response to the current situation at hand, both personally and collectively.

## Living within our means and having a fulfilling life

This book is an attempt to share the ideas, suggestions, wisdom, and stories of others in the hope that you, too, might be inspired to find Upsides to the challenges we all face.

If living *beyond* our means—something we've become pretty good at in the past few decades—is leading us headlong into an unsustainable future and destruction of the environment, then perhaps it's time to figure out how we can live contentedly *within* our means.

If we can truly begin to embrace the realization that **the best things in life are not things**, then what better time than now for each of us to reduce the time spent ruminating about the past (focusing on what we've done or didn't do) and worrying about the future (mistrusting ourselves and life in general)? We can return to the present moment, where true change is possible.

Most of us are fed up with the degree of doom and gloom directed at us daily through the media and other sources regarding the state of our communities, our nation, and the world at large, and we might buffer that by remembering that, in the words of Albert Einstein, "In the middle of difficulty lies opportunity."

There is a golden opportunity surrounding us right now to reflect upon the positive and redeeming aspects of the current state of affairs we're in. The seemingly small changes we make in our thoughts, attitudes, and actions can have powerful effects on our quality of life, our future, and the futures of our children and grandchildren.

The people who are making these inspiring discoveries are ordinary people like you and me. In taking time to reflect and seek out new ways to simplify their lives, they are not only experiencing fulfillment but also a whole new level of engagement with *being alive*. By finding and cultivating Upsides to adversity, they are discovering that life is bringing out the best in them.

## An invitation to find your own Upsides

What about you? Like all of those who contributed to the content of this book, each in his or her own way, you too can begin to shift your daily focus to the multitude of Upsides in your own life—right here, right now.

This is not a "Pollyanna approach" to life, wearing an unreasonably optimistic pair of rose-colored glasses and ignoring the very real stuff happening to us and around us. Rather, the ideas and exercises in this book invite you to find and to nurture the silver linings that can help you deal with everyday problems, reduce stress, and transform your life.

Read on, and remember that every journey begins with one step.

# How to Use This Book

All great masters are chiefly distinguished by the power
of adding a second, a third, and perhaps even
a fourth step in a continuous line.
Many a person has taken the first step.
With every additional step you enhance immensely
the value of your first.

That which we persist in doing becomes easier for us to do;
not that the nature of the thing itself is changed,
but that our power to do is increased.

RALPH WALDO EMERSON

Do what you are going to do.
Don't ponder it.
Don't put it off.
Don't try to do it.
Just do it.
That is the basis of life.

SCOTT SHAW

Is it possible to learn to be more positive? Or to teach yourself to be happier, even when times are tough? What might help you to begin to live this way? Or if you've already begun to shift your focus to the Upside, how could you build upon your progress, simplify the way you live, and create a more fulfilling life?

We've set up this book in a user-friendly way to help you to find and to grow the Upside in your own life. The chapters ahead include inspirational quotes, explorations on a variety of topics, personal stories, questions for consideration, and brief exercises and affirmations to stimulate your imagination and assist you in finding hope, simplicity, and fulfillment in challenging times. We've also included space in each chapter to jot down your own ideas for finding the Upside. Chapter Six, the final one, is designed to help you get started putting the ideas from the book into action in your own life. In addition, this last chapter will assist you in troubleshooting when you run into internal resistance or other roadblocks along the way.

We've also provided further support for finding and living the Upside—a resource section at the back of the book where you'll find links to access an easy-to-use personal assessment tool called the Upside Life Assessment, a collection of selected reading and online resources, and a way to share your stories with others in the Upside community.

This book is meant to be an inspirational set of sparks to ignite your curiosity and exploration, not an exhaustive or academic volume analyzing the extent of the current economic downturn or the factors contributing to the ups and downs of what is happening *out there*.

Recognizing and expanding on the Upsides in life is a process that goes on *in here*: inside your thoughts, perceptions, senses, and feelings about the events in your life and in the world at large. Spending even a little bit of time each day using the tools and concepts offered in this book can make a profound difference in your own life and the impact you have on those around you.

Back in the 1970s, Dr. Maxwell Maltz[2] observed that the human mind, universally, takes almost exactly twenty-one days to adjust to a major life change and that this "21 Day Habit Theory"

---

[2] Maxwell Maltz, M.D., Psycho-Cybernetics (New York: Pocket Books, 1960). First published in 1960, Dr. Maltz's work has been revised and republished in various editions since.

phenomenon still holds true whether the change is negative or positive. The essence of Dr. Maltz's technique is simply to devote fifteen minutes a day to the formation of any habit you wish to establish and to do this faithfully for twenty-one days. By the fourth week, it should actually be harder *not* to engage in the new behavior than it would be to continue doing it. This applies to any type of habit, whether it is a physical practice or a way of perceiving something.

Studies in human motivation and behavior have grown in leaps and bounds since then, but one thing is well known: what we focus on expands. Regardless of whether or not you try the twenty-one-day experiment with any or all of the ideas we present, it's our hope you'll find this book a source of comfort and inspiration in your life, starting today.

Approaching life in a new way requires certain things of us: curiosity, openness, and dedication. But if we keep at it and enlist others to support us as we explore a more expansive way of thinking about and seeing the world, chances are we'll be successful in preventing an economic downturn or any other period of turmoil or adversity from robbing our lives of meaning and fulfillment. Follow the suggestions included in each chapter or make up new ones that fit you.

And finally, we hope that you too will share yours ideas, stories, and suggestions with us. Write to us at: www.upsidematters.org

# CHAPTER ONE

# Cultivating Resilience and Maintaining Optimism in Challenging Times

In times like these, it is good to remember
that there have always been
times like these.

PAUL HARVEY

There are risks and costs to a program of action,
but they are far less than the long-range
risks and costs of comfortable inaction.

JOHN F. KENNEDY

Things do not change.
We change.

HENRY DAVID THOREAU

In a dark time, the eye begins to see.

THEODORE ROETHKE

How do you deal with difficult experiences in your life? What enables you to adjust and eventually recover from challenges such as misfortune, the death of a loved one or loss of a relationship, a serious illness, natural or man-made disasters, and the like?

**Resilience** is a term that grew out of the field of psychology to pinpoint and describe a wonderful ability that all human beings possess, to one degree or another: the capacity to deal positively with stress, adversity, or catastrophe and, in time, to recover from the negative effects of those events.[3]

As it turns out, we not only possess this ability but can learn to expand on it and use it to help us to meet and recover from life's challenges. Further, as we develop the skills to become more resilient, we actually help protect ourselves from the devastating negative effects of future challenges. In essence, as we become more aware of how stressors powerfully affect us and more resourceful in how we respond to them, we enhance our ability to bounce back from negative life experiences.

This is good news, but let's take it even one step further. The term "bouncing back" implies that we'll return to some former state of balance, of relative well-being, or to the person we were *before* the difficulty occurred. In the process of meeting the challenges in life, however, we learn and grow. We are not the same person we were before; we have changed.

Nineteenth-century philosopher Friedrich Nietzsche is credited with that old familiar saying: "What doesn't kill us makes us stronger." Life can make us bitter if we focus on the negative events and outcomes we've experienced. It can also make us wiser and more

---

[3] American Psychological Association Help Center, brochure online, The Road to Resilience, http://www.apahelpcenter.org/featuredtopics/feature.php?id=6

compassionate towards others and ourselves if we learn to look for the Upsides and build on these.

According to the American Psychological Association (APA), resilience is not a trait that a person either has or doesn't have. Resilience involves behaviors, thoughts, and actions that can be learned by anyone. While many factors contribute to how well each of us builds resilience, studies show that the key element involved is having supportive and caring relationships both within and outside of our families. Positive connections with trusted people who offer encouragement when we're down and reassurance when we're feeling shaky help us grow our resilience, especially a belief in our ability to see ourselves through challenging times.

### Barbara's story:
### "Sinking to the bottom and finding solid ground"

In 1992, after eight years of marriage and the fifth and seventh birthdays of my two daughters, my first husband and I separated. I soon found myself in a tiny two-bedroom rental home a mile away from our former residence. I had primary care of my children and an adequate amount of child and spousal support.

Given the young ages of my children and the seven-year gap since my participation in the full-time workforce, I was relying on the understanding that I would have time and options in finding my way back into sustainable employment. When our divorce was finally settled, I would have sufficient means to secure a modest new beginning and create a solid single-parent home for the kids and myself while I explored options and landed a permanent job.

Within two years, however, my ex-spouse went into receivership in his business life and bankruptcy in his personal life. There would be no more formal support, and I could no longer continue renting the home where the girls and I had settled.

With limited retirement savings, a dependable automobile, and firm resolve to create a modest lifestyle I could manage and build upon, I moved to a more urban area of the city known for its "granola lifestyle," tolerance for alternative versions of the nuclear family, and affordable rent.

I felt optimistic and relieved, because these new surroundings would be good for us in re-establishing a life and creating new community. The girls and I could get a dog—something we all wanted—and I could continue to build on part-time work as a counselor.

What I hadn't counted on (and I didn't even see it coming until I was well into it) was how far I would fall emotionally as my financial situation worsened. I was wrapped up in parenting and helping the girls adjust to a new school and neighborhood, trying to remain upbeat and independent with family, friends, and the new people I was meeting who lived near us. Meanwhile, on the inside, the stress, fear, and worry were slowly eroding my patience and hope at ever having what I considered a normal life again.

I don't know that I've ever been successful in describing to others, those who haven't been in a similar situation, what it was like to feel I had become so different from most of the people I knew. They were *out there* in the world, making it. They were getting by. They could support themselves and even build for the future, whereas I was sliding further and further into a sense of isolation and desperation about ever again having enough wits and guts and savvy to hold a professional job in the real-life world. I was an imposter. I was sinking, and I believed it was only a matter of time before the bottom fell out of my world completely. What then?

No one in my former world understood the full extent of my predicament, nor did I attempt to explain it. I was an anomaly in my family and, even if they didn't come right out and say so, my long-time friends were uncomfortable with my situation. I was the living embodiment of their worst fears: ending up a single female parent with no job and few resources. I met a couple of people in my neighborhood who became new friends, and with respect to finances and problems, it seemed some of them were in worse shape than I was. While I was relieved not to have to pretend about my circumstances and struggles, I was secretly afraid I'd end up becoming just like them: closer to the bottom.

Things got worse before they got better—but they *did* eventually get better. I ran out of money, I ended up on social assistance for three months, and I found myself in an employment readiness program funded by the provincial government. I thought things were at their lowest when the doorbell rang in December and a well-meaning friend arrived with a Christmas hamper she and her colleagues at work had created for us. We were their chosen "family in need of Christmas cheer."

My kids, however, were ecstatic. At their young ages, they were greatly impressed by the tangible good will of others at a time of the year when we'd been talking about cutting back and keeping things simple, as in: "It's the thought that counts." After hand-rolling dozens of beeswax candles to give away as Christmas gifts, they now had all the spoils for a roast turkey dinner as well as personal, prettily wrapped gifts to place under the tree.

I'm well aware that the lowest we went, as a family, was nowhere near as low as social and economic circumstances can go. We weren't without food and shelter, and it wasn't long after my start in the re-employment program that I found a full-time job and got back on track with regular paychecks. My earnings were modest, but they paid the bills. Within a year, I was offered a better job by someone I had worked with ten years earlier and, by then, I was mentally and emotionally ready to see myself as capable of making a valuable contribution.

I now understand that I couldn't have gone through those years in any other way. I used to wonder why I wasn't better able to get a grip, pick myself up, and get going again before things got as bad as they did, but I no longer think that way. I did the best I could at the time and learned invaluable lessons in the process.

Two of those lessons I'd like to share here. The first is that my experiences during those years—so many months of so many things falling apart—changed me for the better. I'm no longer as fearful of the multitude of what-ifs about circumstances changing for the worse and requiring me to scale back, losing income, or having to start over. Whatever downturns life brings, my sense is that I'm capable of finding a way to meet and move through them. I've done it before; I can do it again if I need to.

The second thing I now know to be true about myself (and, I suspect, for most of us) is that my core sense of both strength and vulnerability is subject to change without notice and without my permission. There is something inherent in suffering that tempers us and creates a new openness to the pain and suffering of others, if we will let ourselves be changed by our experiences.

Whatever the circumstances in life that trigger a descent towards "the bottom"—loss of a loved one, loss of mobility or income, tragedy or drastic changes in our personal or collective situation—the way *through* will find us if we can muster even a little courage to be honest about our weaknesses, patient with the process, and willing to seek out some friendly support.

While it is always in our best interest to remain open and curious about potential Upsides in any situation, there will be times in life when it's just not possible to push forward in all-wheel drive. There's value, learning, and growing in giving ourselves permission to feel the depth of the losses in our lives and to allow time to grieve.

I have things mostly together in my life at the present moment and am doing the best I can to take care of myself so that I remain physically healthy, emotionally resilient, and mentally positive in my orientation towards life. My circumstances, however, could change dramatically at any moment. It is the care and feeding of my spiritual nature—my faith in the unseen intelligence that sustains life—that allows me to live in a relatively calm manner in the midst of potential and sudden change. This is the sense of "solid ground" I carry within me.

**Optimism** is a word we hear often, in many forms. A person is described as being optimistic about an outcome (possessing an expectation that things will turn out in a favorable way), for instance, or as being a born optimist if they consistently tend to expect the best of life and of other people.

### Steve's story:
### "Born pessimists have to work at being optimists"

I remember the moment when I made a significant shift in perspective about the dramatic economic downturn. It was a sunny fall day in 2008 and I was sitting on my sofa looking out a window into a section of forest near my home. I was feeling tentative, worried, and anxious about the future. I had spent the past year putting major effort into creating a new company focused on working with people in the second half of life, and now that I was approaching its launch, the reality of financial downturn was all around me—in the headlines, in my bank statements, and in the themes of most of the conversations taking place with friends, clients, and in my community. What a time to start a new business! It seemed like my timing couldn't be worse.

Another thing that was getting to me at the time was a sense of pressure to come up with ways to help create change in the current economic situation. I was becoming preoccupied with what needed to happen and how it could be done so that the world could begin to be set right and I could start to relax.

That afternoon, it suddenly dawned on me that maybe this was the *perfect* time for a new venture, especially if it was in some way able to help people cope with these difficult times. I was stunned at the thought. Though I couldn't account for where this notion had come from, there was no denying its momentous impact on me. With amazing clarity, I began to see exactly what I was doing to myself as I sat there engaging in doom-and-gloom thinking, which was not only unhelpful to getting on with my work but was contributing to a sense of helplessness and a depressing mood.

I realized I'd gone into autopilot mode, defaulting to an old tendency under stress to revert back into thinking like a born pessimist: that if something goes wrong, it's probably my fault; that it will probably last a long time; that I won't be able to make much of a difference; that it's going to undermine everything else; and on and on. Within seconds, I saw not only how I had slipped into this mindset, but also how I could pull out the ladder of cognitive skills I'd built over the years to climb back out.

These realizations all took place within a matter of minutes, but they were profound enough to ignite a shift in my thinking and a refocusing of my efforts. The result was an entirely new series of creative ideas, including *The Upside to the Downturn* website (now www.upsidematters. org), as well as a weekly web-based column called *Starting Your Week on the Upside*, and the impetus for many collaborative interactions with others leading to a number of other exciting new projects, including this book.

I'm not embarrassed to admit that I'm a born pessimist and a learned optimist. I've found that I constantly have to look at and manage my thoughts in order to keep things in proper perspective. My old tendency is to blow things out of proportion and get hung up on what's not possible or probable, but I have successfully learned how to catch myself when I do this. I've also learned how to challenge the negative thinking in ways that help me to see the potential positive aspects and how I might be able to follow up with specific steps and actions. All this is usually easier said than done, but for me, it's critically important to keep myself on track.

## Slowing down and shifting into neutral

What has worked for me over time is the applied analogy of working a muscle in the body so that it gains strength: if I regularly work on shifting out of negative thinking and unhelpful moods, then I'll get better and stronger at it over time. Basically, my approach is fairly simple. When stressed or noticing a pessimistic thought or feeling arising within, I try my best to halt my current line of thinking, go inward (shift my focus to what's going on in my body) by becoming aware of my breath, and give myself permission to *slow down*. The goal for me is to get quiet and shift into neutral by focusing on my breathing and my body for a few minutes in this calm way. What I've noticed (thankfully!) is that this process begins to relax the content and quality of my thoughts into a more positive overall focus.

Even if I don't have the solution to a problem or can't yet see the best next step to take, just the act of slowing down and breathing—without needing to think at all—begins to lift the feeling of heaviness or of being stuck. I'm able to create space between the perceived problem and myself, and I really do "come to my senses." I've noticed that doing this in nature or with soft soothing music in the background helps me to let go into this process more easily, especially when my thoughts or emotions have a strong grip on me. This is an ongoing work-in-progress, but I'm happy to report that with time and diligence, I can now describe myself a much more optimistic person than I used to be.

## Taking good care of myself

Another insight I had at the time was that with respect to having an impact on the macro-issues of the 2009 economic mess, there was very little within my personal control. I would therefore have to rely on hope, trusting that people way smarter and wiser than me would get our banking and financial systems, as well as the economy, back on track.

I realized, however, that there are a number of areas of my life that I *do* have control over and that these affect my health, well-being, and outlook. These include making a personal commitment to eating a healthy diet, getting a good night's sleep, breathing lots of fresh air, and maintaining a regular exercise program. In addition, I have to remember not to beat myself up if and when I get off track. Instead, I need to continue doing my best to get back on my learned-optimism program and taking good care of myself.

I also find it important to control the flow and content of the news media I expose myself to. I no longer read a paper or watch the news on TV, for example. Instead, I go online and read only the stories that I find helpful, hopeful, or inspiring. I've started downloading podcasts of interest and listening to them while walking or exercising.

One further new thing I've implemented is to not open my financial statements with the daily mail, as I did in the past. I set these aside for a time when I'm in the right frame of mind for reviewing such matters. I don't put them off for long, but I do put them off until a time when I know I can be as optimistic as possible.

I feel that maintaining healthy emotional and mental states, particularly in our current times, is critical to well-being. Most importantly, I've found that I do best when I surround myself with basically optimistic and supportive people so that I can maintain my strength and perspective as well as be there for others.

According to Dr. Martin Seligman, who has written about optimism for many years, Steve's experience of sitting on the sofa thinking about worst possible outcomes and believing his thoughts to be true is a common experience. Most of this kind of thinking—the unhelpful kind—goes on just beneath the surface of our awareness. It's kind of like background music; we tend to let it play on and don't pay it much attention.

When Steve caught himself in this kind of thinking and began to challenge the negative thoughts that were getting him discouraged, he was using a skill called **disputing**. Psychologists use this term to describe the process of treating the negative or fear-based things we say to ourselves as we would a person in the external world whose goal in life is to make us miserable. If someone were standing in front of us making false accusations, we would likely dispute them. We can learn to do the same with ourselves, on the inside.

It seems so obvious, doesn't it? But how often do we stop to really listen to the things we're telling ourselves as we go through our day, especially when we notice we're in a gloomy mood or feeling defeated about someone or something that matters to us?

Seligman, in his book *Learned Optimism*,[4] writes that a degree of pessimism does have its place in situations where the downside risks are unacceptable, especially in a business setting. Such risks need to be carefully assessed before decisions are made.

But for the majority of situations in our everyday lives, we can remind ourselves that we are not *helpless* when facing most circumstances or our own thoughts. Instead, we can see a difficult situation as a temporary setback or a challenge that we can handle and work through, using our own effort and abilities. We can also turn to others we trust to gain support and encouragement while we explore ways to meet and overcome the obstacle confronting us.

Change is a part of living. Its one thing we can count on. As we develop confidence in our ability to work towards solutions to the challenges that life brings our way, we begin to trust our instincts, build resilience, and expect that good things, too, will come our way.

---

[4] Martin E. P. Seligman, Learned Optimism: How to Change Your Mind and Your Life (New York: Pocket Books, 1998). See Chapter Six, and see related article at: http://www.egtoday.com/optimism/seligman.html

### Karen's story:
### "I Believe...."

I believe that our society will learn to live more with less because of this downturn.
I believe that change is here.
I believe that we are going to put the "eco" back in economics.
I believe that families and friends everywhere are reconnecting with nature and with one another.
I believe Art and Story (both free!) are essential to healthy people and societies.
I believe that peace is everywhere.
I believe that God provides.
I believe in an abundance mentality.
I believe in me.

*Submitted in late 2009 at the height of the of the economic downturn*

# Questions for reflection

- What kinds of events have been most stressful for me? How have those events typically affected me?

- Do I have a habit of resorting to pessimistic thinking when confronted with a challenge or problem? How do I know this or notice this? What else have I noticed about my responses to stressful events in my life?

- Can I think of a time when I caught myself thinking pessimistically? Did I dispute the negative things I was telling myself or telling someone else? Why not?

- Do I tend to turn to others when I need encouragement and support? Has this been helpful? When and how?

- Have I been able to overcome obstacles in my life to date? How did I do this?

- Is my outlook on life more positive than it used to be? How do I account for this?

- Who comes to mind when I think of a person I know or know about who handles stressful situations in a positive way? What is it I've noticed about how this person meets challenges? Can I see myself taking similar actions in my own life? What, if anything, would be in the way of me doing this?

## Exercise 1 – An exercise in Finding the Upside

### Step 1 – Define the problem

Take a moment to think of three events or situations in your life today that are stressful and have you caught up in feelings of frustration, helplessness, fear, or hopelessness. Write each of these down, working with your description until you get each situation into a brief, clear focus—for example: "My hours have been cut back at work, and I have less money coming in every two weeks. I'm worried that there will be nothing left over after I pay the bills."

Stressful situations in my current life:

1. _____
2. _____
3. _____

### Step 2 – Find an Upside to the situation

Allow yourself to step back from the troublesome feelings surrounding the issue and come up with one or two new and potentially positive things that might come from or with this circumstance. Here's an example: "Other people are going through this too and surviving on less money. I can take a closer look at my income and expenses and see where things actually stand. I can think about what to do with the extra time I now have and discuss with my family ways to make do with less money and more time."

If you find yourself having difficulty stepping back from your thoughts and feelings about the situation in order to explore new ideas, read on to Chapter Three and try the exercise in present moment awareness at the end of the chapter. As you learn to relax and let go of the grip of your mind, you will open yourself up to new ways to view and change the situations in your life that cause you distress .

Possible Upsides for me to consider:

1. _____
2. _____
3. _____
4. _____
5. _____

## Affirmations

Affirmations are statements that, when stated or held in quiet thought, can foster positive thinking and cultivate change in desired directions.

- In any situation, I can always find ways to take action to deal with the problems that confront me. I will be more successful at this when I catch myself engaging in pessimistic thinking and dispute the negative things I'm saying to myself.

- I can turn to others I trust when I need support and encouragement. I can also rely on my own abilities and experience to meet the challenges in my life.

- While things may be difficult right now, I will come through this. I won't let myself blow this out of proportion.
- It's okay to let myself feel strong emotions when things get me down. It's also okay to set them aside or avoid them sometimes so that I can keep on with my day in a productive way.
- It's good for me to take care of myself, even when things are stressful and there are problems facing me. By taking the time to eat well, exercise, do things I enjoy, and relax, I am helping my mind and body to build resilience, which I can call upon when challenges come my way.

## Notes to myself _____

# CHAPTER TWO

# Spending Less, Choosing Wisely and Enjoying More

If you follow your bliss,
you will always have your bliss, money or not.
If you follow money, you may lose it,
and you will have nothing.

JOSEPH CAMPBELL

Whatever you have, spend less.
Without frugality, none can be rich,
and with it,
very few would be poor.

SAMUEL JOHNSON

Making a living is not the same thing
as making a life.

MAYA ANGELOU

Let's focus on the insights that can be drawn from challenging economic times and consider potential changes in personal perspective and behavior. We'll start with a version of a familiar parable that illustrates just how easily we can lose sight of what really matters in life.

---

### A timeless story:
### "The Mexican fisherman and the MBA"

A vacationing tourist—a successful and educated businessman—was standing at the pier of a small, coastal Mexican village when a modest boat pulled up to the dock. The boat contained a local fisherman and several large yellowfin tuna.

The businessman complimented the Mexican fisherman on the quality of his fish and asked how long it took to catch them. The fisherman replied, "Only a little while."

The businessman then asked why the fisherman didn't stay out longer to catch more fish. The fisherman said he had enough to support his family's immediate needs. Curious, the businessman said, "But what do you do with the rest of your time?" The fisherman answered: "I sleep late, fish a little, play with my children, take a siesta with my wife, Maria, and stroll into the village each evening where I sip wine and play guitar with my amigos. I have a full and busy life, señor."

The businessman scoffed. "I have an Ivy League MBA and I could help you. Here's what you should do: spend more time fishing and with the proceeds, buy a bigger boat. With the added catch from the bigger boat you could buy several boats. In time, you would have a whole fleet of fishing boats. Instead of selling your catch to a middleman, you could sell directly to the processor and eventually open your own cannery. You would control the product, processing, and distribution. You could eventually escape this small fishing village and move to Mexico City, then perhaps Los Angeles and eventually New York City, where you would run your expanding enterprise."

The fisherman paused and then spoke: "But señor, how long will all this take?"

To which the businessman replied, "Fifteen to twenty years."

"But what then, señor?"

The businessman laughed and said, "That's the best part! When the time is right, you would announce an IPO and sell your company stock to the public and become very rich. You would make millions."

"Millions, señor? Then what?" asked the fisherman.

The businessman answered, "Then you would retire. You could move to a small, coastal fishing village where you would sleep late, fish a little, play with your kids, take a siesta with your wife, and stroll to the village in the evenings where you could sip wine and play your guitar with your amigos."

The fisherman, now smiling, looked up and said, "Isn't that what I'm already doing?"

-Author Unknown

---

There's the essence of the economic mess we got ourselves into as the first decade of the twenty-first century was ending! As a society and as individuals, we believed that more was better, that bigger was also better, and that increased spending brought increased wealth. The result was a devastating wake-up call.

## Taking a look in the mirror

As the economic problems compounded in late 2008 and early 2009, we quickly looked for someone to blame for the Great Recession. We pointed fingers at the global governmental and institutional lending policies and practices. Frantic to track individual and corporate greed and corruption, we cast an incriminating eye at lending companies such as AIG and money managers like Bernie Madoff.

We also realized that as individuals, we needed to look in the mirror. Many of us have recently benefited from time spent taking a look at our personal spending patterns and life priorities.

As a society, we'd bought into the concept of having whatever we wanted whenever we wanted it. We have been conditioned to believe that living in comfort is the same as having a full and fulfilling life. In the long run, this approach is not sustainable or even satisfying for most of us.

A 1998 PBS broadcast entitled *Affluenza*[5] did a brilliant job of examining the high cost of achieving the extravagant lifestyle we collectively enjoy and the extent to which our lives and lifestyles are out of balance. The show drove home the point that Americans, who made up only 5 percent of the world's population at the time, use nearly a third of global resources and produce almost half its hazardous waste. The show's producers were quick to point out that, as they said, the American Dream is no bargain.

Author and thought leader Hale Dwoskin commented on the affluenza concept in this way: "Everything about our culture is designed to make us feel that we do not have enough or that we are

---

[5]  PBS Television first aired Affluenza: The Epidemic of Overconsumption on July 7, 1998. See http://www.pbs.org/kcts/affluenza/

not enough as we are. This creates all sorts of distortions, including always wanting more and over consuming."[6]

## Having enough

In a beautifully written book entitled *Enough: True Measures of Money, Business and Life*,[7] John C. Bogle lays out a powerful argument for the macro and personal changes required for our economy to recover and for individuals to become more aware and individually responsible. He begins the book by detailing a story about two legendary authors: novelist Kurt Vonnegut and Joseph Heller of *Catch-22* fame. While attending an exclusive party at a megamillionaire's Long Island mansion, the two writers were both gazing at the opulence surrounding them. In those pre-meltdown days, Vonnegut turned to Heller and commented he suspected that the owner of the house made more money in one afternoon than Heller would make in a lifetime of worldwide royalties for *Catch-22*. There was a short silence, then Heller looked back at Vonnegut and said, "Yes, perhaps, but I have enough."

What would our personal and collective world be like if our focus were on appreciation, gratitude, and satisfaction in having enough? Put another way, is it possible to have a good or even a great life and live within or below our means? We believe the answer is a very definite and much-needed "YES!"

Some sobering and yet hopeful research on the concept of enough was conducted recently at Harvard University by social

---

[6]  "The Seven Deadly Sins: How Over-Consumption Hurts You and the Planet and How to End 'Affluenza'," February 12, 2009, Sedona Method wellness newsletter at http://www.sedona.com/over-consumption.aspx/

[7]  John C. Bogle, Enough: *True Measures of Money, Business, and Life* (Hoboken, N.J.: John Wiley & Sons, 2008).

psychologist Daniel Gilbert. In his book *Stumbling on Happiness*,[8] Gilbert reports that the largest spike in self-reported life satisfaction and happiness occurs when an individual has basic needs met for shelter, food, and sustainable employment. Beyond this level, there is a very poor relationship between more money and more happiness, meaning that once our basic needs are met (having enough), additional wealth (having more) will not make us any happier.

The implications of this are profound. "People who earn $50,000 per year are much happier than those who earn $10,000 per year," writes Gilbert, "but people who earn $5 million per year are not much happier than those who earn $100,000 per year." [9]

Similarly, Tim Kasser, author of *The High Price of Materialism*,[10] found in his research that people who are more materialistic are less happy and have less satisfying social interactions than those who are less invested in, as they say, keeping up with the Joneses. True happiness, according to his data, comes from meaningful experiences such as growing as a person and feeling connected to friends and family.

Ed Diener from the University of Illinois and the Gallup Organization and Martin E.P. Seligman from the University of Pennsylvania found that having more disposable income can actually distort one's sense of life satisfaction.

Among the conclusions in their seminal research study, "Beyond Money: Toward an Economy of Well-Being," is this: "With increasing income there are expanding aspirations and a sense that there is always one more thing out there that people absolutely have to have.

[8]   Daniel Gilbert, *Stumbling On Happiness* (New York: Vintage Books, 2006).

[9]   Gilbert, *Stumbling on Happiness*, p. 217.

[10]  Tim Kasser, *The High Price of Materialism* (Cambridge, MA: The MIT Press, 2002).

Economic success falls short as a measure of well-being, in part because materialism can negatively influence well-being."[11]

The late Joseph Campbell captured the essence of the futility of striving after more: "Many of us climb the ladder of success only to realize we have the ladder on the wrong wall."[12]

## When net worth becomes self-worth

Since we tend to focus on what we measure in our life and work, we pay a heavy and distorted price when we limit our definition of personal success to our net worth. For many of us, our sense of *self-worth* becomes firmly and dangerously entwined in our estimation of our net worth. The results can be devastating.

This was powerfully illustrated in a personal conversation in early 2009 between one of the authors of this book and an official of the Coroner's Office in a large U.S. city. The official described an alarming increase in white-collar suicides since the onset of the recession. He was referring to a rise in the premeditated deaths of people who lost significant amounts of money and who strongly associated their net worth with their personal value as human beings.

Suicide notes and follow-up conversations with the affected families revealed the despair and demoralization the now-deceased individuals had suffered as a result of no longer having financial wealth. They found life unbearable.

---

[11]  Edward Diener and Martin E. P. Seligman, "Beyond Money: Toward an Economy of Well-Being," *Psychological Science in the Public Interest*, Vol. 5, No. 1 (June 2004), pp. 1-31.

[12]  Joseph J. Campbell (1904-1987) was an American mythology professor, orator and writer best known for his work in the fields of mythology and comparative religion and his numerous bestselling books. His reference to climbing the ladder of success can be found in his book *The Power of Myth*, which is based on his conversations with Bill Moyers. It has been reissued in several editions since it was first published (Doubleday, 1988; Anchor Books, 1991).

This describes a very sad state of affairs that is affecting all of us collectively. It became a powerful motivator for creating this book and the related website and resources.

If we, as a society, stay focused on the downturn and downsides of what we see as the bad stuff happening to us and to others, where will it lead? Life will always bring the good (the circumstances we like) along with the bad (the events we would rather not experience or deal with). How can we get off this stressful roller coaster?

## Report card on self-worth

We propose that a revised, personal success report card is needed. Our financial portfolios, the size of our homes, and the number and quality of our possessions certainly factor into how we sum up our sense of personal wealth. In determining our true personal worth, however, we could begin to place *at least as much* weight (and hopefully more) on these other assets:

- our health and well-being;
- the quality of our relationships;
- our capacity to be resilient and optimistic;
- our ability to find happiness in a more simplified way of living, making wise decisions that lead to spending less and enjoying life more;
- our willingness to clear out the clutter that is adversely impacting our living environments, our mental and physical functioning, our emotional states, and our relationships with others;
- our unique interests, strengths and passions; and
- our willingness to give back and contribute to the lives of others.

Spending less, making wise financial decisions, and enjoying life more are all attractive propositions, particularly during tough economic times.

## Are we ready, willing, and able to change?

The recession that officially began in the fall of 2008 was declared over, technically, in June 2009, but the recession's effects will linger for decades. High unemployment, high rates of foreclosures and unsteady consumer confidence are effects that will keep local and larger economies struggling for a long time.

All the while, a number of trends have been emerging since the height of the recession—positive Upside trends relating to consumer behavior, spending, and savings:

- Reduction of personal debt
- Significant increases in personal savings
- Embracing frugal behaviours and lifestyle

## Personal debt

Credit card debt has been reduced dramatically. As of late 2010, credit card debt has dropped to an eight-year low. More borrowers are also making their payments on time.

People are discovering that this is not only a good time to reduce personal debt but also an important time to work on paying off heavy debt loads. This includes people on tight budgets who are finding ways to reduce existing debt, slowly but surely, mostly through setting priorities on their spending. They are putting more focus on necessities and less on luxuries.

The net effect of personal debt being reduced is that with a healthier financial situation, one's credit ratings can be improved. This will be particularly beneficial for fiscally minded consumers looking to borrow in the future, since banks and lenders have severely restricted their lending practices, making it tougher to get loans without above average credit.

## Money in the bank: a word about savings

A few modern misconceptions about saving money have been shattered during the economic pullback. Do these sound familiar?

- I don't really need to save. I can easily borrow money at cheap interest rates when I need it.
- My investments and my home are my savings. The stock market has glitches but it always goes up. I'll be fine.
- The world is so unpredictable these days, so why worry about down the road? I'm comfortable today, and I'll face tomorrow, tomorrow.

The recession has served as a wake-up call, and statistics say we are getting the message. The *Wall Street Journal* on June 27, 2009, claimed that U.S. consumers are now saving more of their incomes than at any time since 1993. The paper called this a major shift toward frugality that may well be one of the lasting effects of the 2008-09 recession.

The online blog *Get Rich Slowly* confirms this rise, noting that the personal saving rate—an economic term for disposable income that's not used immediately to buy goods and services—jumped from 0.4 percent in 2007 to a dramatic 7.2 percent for most of the latter half of 2009 and continuing between 5 percent and 6 percent into late 2010.

The Bureau of Economic Analysis, an agency of the U.S. Department of Commerce, tracks historical data on the personal saving rate and provides monthly updates on the status of U.S. income and saving. J. D. Roth in his blog writes: "For decades, the personal saving rate hovered at about seven or eight percent. It would spike into the teens during times of economic turmoil but then settle at seven or eight percent when things returned to normal. During the early 1990s, however, the personal saving rate began to drop. For the past ten years, it's mostly been two percent or one percent or close to zero."[13]

However we managed to do it, as a culture we gradually dropped the savings ball and are just now starting to take the game seriously again. Debt has us in a stranglehold, limiting our choices in the present and the future. To turn things around and save successfully, we need to spend more wisely. The math is simple: the less we spend, the more we potentially have left over to save.

As with anything else in life, balance is critical. By balancing our enjoyment of everyday life in the here and now with a prudent approach to our financial future (including an adequate safety net along the way), we limit the stress of the unknown. When it comes to money, small changes and good habits can make all the difference.

But it's not often easy to turn around our patterns with money. In her recent book, *Spent: Break the Buying Obsession and Discover Your True Worth*,[14] Sally Palaian, Ph.D., stresses the urgency of the

---

[13] The popular website/blog *Get Rich Slowly: Personal Finance that Makes Cents* (www.getrichslowly.org/ blog) is not by a financial professional but by "average guy" J.D. Roth, who found himself deep in debt and devoted himself to the study of sensible personal finance. He offers practical philosophy and advice on getting rich slowly.

[14] Sally Palaian, *Spent: Break the Buying Obsession and Discover Your True Worth* (Center City, MN: Hazelden Publishing, 2009).

societal challenge upon us. That challenge, she says, is to learn more about our relationship with money so we can find the balance be-tween financial survival and personal fulfillment.

The purpose of her book is to downsize this quest for balance from the societal to the individual level, helping readers come to grips with their personal relationship with money and the issues that get in the way of achieving financial balance. She then establishes a gradual, practical plan for financial recovery and lasting, positive change.

According to Palaian, it's no wonder money problems are so prevalent in our culture. "Lack of financial education, coupled with the complexity of modern financial survival," she writes, "is a fast formula for growing financial dysfunctions—a breeding ground for problems with money, spending, and self-control. It's no surprise that so many people have so much trouble with money management."

## Embracing frugality

In his book *The Cheapskate Next Door*,[15] Jeff Yeager captures the current tone and insights of people committed to living simpler, less consumer-driven lives without feeling they are sacrificing. He spent two-and-a-half years traveling the United States to answer two questions:

- How can some people live not only within their means, but substantially *below* their means—even when their incomes are often less than the national average?
- How can some of those same people report feeling happier because of their thrift and frugality?

---

[15] Jeff Yeager, *The Cheapskate Next Door: The Surprising Secrets of Americans Living Happily Below Their Means* (New York: Broadway Books, 2010).

Yeager interviewed more than three hundred individuals and came to some of the following conclusions about people looking to simplify their lives and live more frugally:

- They despise debt and have found creative ways to eliminate it from their lives.
- They are able to differentiate between "needs" and "wants" and between "affordability" and "borrow-ability".
- Fewer than 10 percent talked about needing a written household budget. As one person put it, "We live our budget—it's second nature—we don't waste time writing about it."
- And more than nine out of ten say that they think, worry, and stress-out about money *less*, not more, than others.

Two additional insights particularly stood out from his interviews:

- Frugal people are often immune to buyer's remorse. Nearly 90 percent of those surveyed reported they "never" or "rarely" regret a purchase. Most shoppers eventually regret nearly 80 percent of the discretionary items they buy.
- Frugal people embrace the concept that the best things in life *aren't* things. As Yeager put it, "Social science has shown that Stuff tends to disappoint us over time, but experiences—how we spend our time—is what adds true value and meaning to life.... Frugal people value their time, and the things they can do with it, more than money, and the things they can buy with it."

## Maintaining the momentum and addressing the voices in our head

Will we ever return to a pattern of overspending and generally over-consumptive ways? Or will there be an outbreak of "new normal behavior" that reflects a more modest baseline of increased financial restraint and commitment to living within our means? The answer is likely both.

We humans tend to be creatures of habit. We are prone to return to familiar ways of behavior even when there is compelling internal and/or external evidence that a change in behavior would be beneficial. The difficulty experienced by smokers who want to quit is a common example.

Yet others among us are able to adopt new behaviors and do it permanently. The catalyst for such change quite often occurs during times of crisis and challenge, when we are shaken out of our usual comfort zones and are moved to respond in entirely new ways. Not everyone, however, is able or willing to sustain these changes.

Take any two people who suffer a near-fatal heart attack, for example. During the rehabilitation phase, the first might resolve to make and maintain lifelong, health-promoting changes in diet, exercise regime, and stress-reduction behaviors. They're successful at it. The other, who started out with good intentions, soon reverts to the old familiar routines and lifestyle patterns that contributed to the health crisis.

Which would you be in this situation? If you're honest in considering this, you'll likely need a long pause to consider your previous level of success at changing deeply embedded habits. There are so many influencing factors to take into account.

How does this relate to changing consumer behavior? Ran Kivetz, a professor of marketing at Columbia Business School, has done extensive research on consumer psychology.[16] He argues that consumers' brains lack a line that separates spending from saving.

---

[16] An interview with Columbia Business School professor of marketing Ran Kivetz is included in the *Bloomberg BusinessWeek* cover story by Devin Leonard entitled "The New Abnormal" (July 29, 2010).

Instead, we practice a certain amount of thrift so that we can justify blowing a large sum frivolously.

Kivetz says the recent downturn has made consumer thinking even more conflicted. In the short run, we feel good when we save. In the long run, we tend to regret the denial of a spending outlet. We "feel guilty" about spending, according to Kivetz, which can lead to more irrational purchasing.

And that, he says, is exactly what's happening now. Consumers were quick to reduce spending when the recession arrived. Then the recession lasted longer than expected, and the new abnormal set in. The economy started to improve. Then it appeared to worsen. Kivetz says there is only so long we can suppress our need to spend. Life has to have some normalcy: "I have to have some luxuries."

What can we do to suppress our need to spend and increase our need to save?

National Public Radio economic commentator Beth Kobliner shared some sage advice about "making it easy to save and harder to spend."[17] She calls it the Do-It-Yourself Bailout. Her practical and commonsense suggestions, backed up by behavior research, include the following:

1. **Set your cell phone or computer to remind you to save.** A 2010 study by economists from Harvard and Yale and co-authored by Jonathan Zinman of Dartmouth found that bank customers who were reminded of their savings goals with monthly text messages stashed away 6 percent more money than those who didn't receive reminders. So set your calendar to remind you of your goals. Use Post-it notes, refrigerator magnets, screensavers, mobile alerts—whatever

---

[17] Beth Kobliner teamed up with the national radio show "The Takeaway" to give Americans a way to bail themselves out of their personal financial troubles. Her 10-step plan, the "Do-It-Yourself Bailout", can be found on her website: http://www.bethkobliner.com/the-diy-bailout/

works for you. More simply, contact your bank and ask them to withdraw automatically out of your checking account a set amount after each pay period—say, $50 or $100 a month—and have it transferred to savings.

2. Don't let your computer make it too easy to spend. With popular websites like Gilt Groupe, Groupon, and RueLaLa offering deep discounts to your favorite retailers, you don't even have to leave your desk to blow money on shopping sprees. Erase your credit card information from tempting sites, don't allow them to save your passwords, and delete bookmarks to places where you're likely to spend. But do use sites like www.bankrate.com to get the lowest rate on credit cards and www.billshrink.com to see if there's a better cell phone or wireless plan for you.

3. **Use cash not plastic.** A classic 2001 study from MIT found that people were willing to pay twice as much for the same items when they paid with credit cards compared to when they paid with cash. So stick to an all-cash diet. Another 2008 study by Priya P. Raghubir of NYU and Joydeep Srivastava of the University of Maryland, found that people tend to treat credit cards and gift cards like "monopoly money"—meaning that plastic feels less real and people are less careful about overspending with it. Take out a fixed amount of cold, hard, cash from the ATM each week and hold yourself to that sum of money to get you through the week.

4. **Check your emotions.** Research from British psychologists done in 2009 and other studies by American psychologists show that we're willing to spend more money when emotions run rampant. In fact, in one famous study from Carnegie Mellon, participants who'd been shown a tearjerker about a dying parent were willing to fork over almost four times more for a bottle of water,

compared to people who'd been shown a documentary about the Great Barrier Reef. Save your shopping for your mellow moods.

5. **Shop with frugal friends.** Studies show that friends (and even friends-of-friends) influence everything from how much you weigh to how much you smoke. And at least some unpublished preliminary research seems to show that friends can influence how you can spend as well. Next time you're planning a big-ticket purchase, bring a frugal pal shopping with you. Take your spendthrift friends on a run instead.

There are many other useful resources available to help you assess your financial circumstances and determine your plan for change. Some of these resources are low-cost or no-cost, such as those offered by government agencies and websites or by your local bank, countless books, and reputable online resources. We have suggested a number of these in the resources section of our website (www.upsidematters.org/premium).

## Going Forward

There is no doubt that many people are suffering terribly from the global economic situation, the austerity measures in many countries, and the fears and resentments that are coming out. At the same time, knowledgeable and insightful sources are speculating that one Upside of the 2008 recession may in fact be its duration.

In other words, the longer these times of sober restraint continue, the more likely it is that long-term, positive, sustainable changes will occur at all levels of our society. As we accept the grave reality of the circumstances we're in and will continue to be in, personally and collectively, and as we come to realize that the old ways we've been living are part of the overall problem, we can begin to see the advantages of sustaining a simpler and more balanced life.

Maureen (not her real name) is a poignant example. Maureen was a participant in a one-day workshop of Steve's entitled "Having a Magnificent Life and Living within Your Means." At the end of the afternoon, she came forward and shared with Steve that she had lost the majority of her life savings after investing nearly all her resources with a well-known (and later jailed) financial broker.

While the impact of the sudden loss was a huge shock to her at first, it was nowhere near as devastating as the death of her husband the previous year. A self-described survivor, Maureen decided her key priority was to take care of her family, doing what she could to help them feel safe and secure. There would be time later for her anger and grief at the financial fallout.

Shortly after the discovery of their shared losses, several of her similarly affected family members decided to cut expenses and move in together. Maureen quickly realized how surprisingly enriching it was for everyone to be together under the same roof and striving toward common goals. Working together, they became more frugal in their spending habits and, in their shared experience, began to find growing energy to meet the challenges they faced. The family discovered a sense of enjoyment in seeking out bargains, all the while making continual adjustments of individual priorities in ways that held personal meaning for each person as they made progress toward the established goals of the group.

One of Maureen's biggest *aha!* moments was when her granddaughter, calculator in hand, caught Maureen unthinkingly adding several items to the grocery cart, items that were not on their shopping list. "Grandma," the girl exclaimed, "do you *realize* what you just spent in the past minute?" A flabbergasted Maureen placed the unnecessary items back on the shelf, her awareness and behavior permanently altered.

Maureen admits there are things her family members miss from their earlier and more financially cushioned lives, but she is quick to add that the new kinds of riches introducing themselves into their lives as a result of their financial crisis *far* outweigh the related losses.

Maureen and her kin strongly believe that the changes in attitudes, beliefs, and behavior they are experiencing will probably be permanent, and she believes they are all better people as a result.

### Stephen's story: "More bang for the Bach, and finding joy for the price of a song"

I'm not feeling that old-style patriotism here in the U.S.A. since consumers in the U.S., who are responsible for 70 percent of their GDP, have gone from spending more than they earn to saving at a rate of 4 percent. Have we forgotten the words of President George W. Bush, who rallied us in our despair after September 11th? "Keep shopping," he said.

Did you buy that, back then? And whether or not you did, what are you buying now?

Here's a report on my personal contribution to the GDP: a few months ago, I bought the classical guitar sheet music for J. S. Bach's *Fugue in A minor*. It cost me $12.95, plus $3.50 for shipping and handling, for a total of $16.45.

I am still learning this piece. Every night, when I take out my guitar, I have a conversation with a genius. With each phrase, Bach tells me how to arrange notes in a sequence that creates startling beauty.

So far, my investment has cost me a little over eighteen cents an evening. But it's the return on investment that has me so ecstatic. In 1969, I gave up the idea of being a professional concert guitarist. I had my reasons: I didn't like the life of solitary practice, I had good but not great chops, and performing was scary. So, for forty years, I gave up daily practice. Now, I practice every night. I'm in love with Bach, and I've reclaimed a treasure from my past.

In these recession days, when many of us have more time on our hands, what can we each find, dust off, revive, or begin that brings simple joy to others and ourselves?

Maybe this kind of inquiry will guide us to a more sane and humane economy. That would be a magnificent Upside to the downturn.

---

## Living (well) within our means

Responsible spending and consuming are key drivers in a successful economy. We can't escape the need to purchase goods and services—and, indeed, this is a necessary component in local and global economic recovery.

Do you believe that it's completely possible to live a full and satisfying life within your actual financial means? Maybe you're already successfully doing this. If not, can you imagine this being possible? Could you achieve it once you've realistically examined your needs and adjusted your priorities according to your own determination of what's important and how much is *enough*?

Our society is at a critical crossroads. It's hard to predict where we'll end up. As we come into more conscious awareness and control of our spending habits and lifestyles, we'll be better attuned to the meaning of true wealth, fulfillment, and life satisfaction.

What we each have to offer is our own personal behavior and commitment to long-term change. Are you ready for the challenge?

### Steve's story: "Saving for my dream home"

In the spring of 1991, I was part of a small group of people who purchased a beautiful piece of property on one of the magnificent Gulf Islands in British Columbia, Canada. Among this ecstatic group of new landowners, I know I wasn't the only one who felt that this was a dream come true. None of us could have afforded to buy the land on our own.

Building a home on my portion of the land took fifteen years because I held to my standard—imprinted on me by my parents since my earliest childhood—to spend only when I had enough money saved to do so. I kept my small rented apartment on the mainland and commuted to the island property on weekends and during summer vacations.

At first, there was no running water or electricity at my island paradise. I built an outhouse and hauled jugs of water from my generous neighbors. Back and forth from the city, I carried a 12-volt battery to supply enough charge in the trailer to power a small refrigerator and some lights at night. Although it was rustic, I loved being on the land and dreaming of the time I would be able to build my home.

I realize I'm not the norm in today's society because I have never bought on credit and have never had a mortgage. As the sole owner of my own small business, I have experienced both robust and lean years with respect to income. I prefer these fluctuations to the trade-offs I would have to make if I lived a more traditional life involving loans and lines of credit. I never wanted to be in the situation where I would have to accept a work contract I didn't really want in order to keep up with a mortgage payment.

For so many years, I felt like an oddball about my personal financial convictions. In fact, it was not until the arrival of this recession—and the outpouring of stories revealing the darker side of the structure of our economy— that I felt comfortable even sharing my story with others.

Now, I'm aware of so many Upsides to the way I went about creating my first home, even if it did take me fifteen years:

- Taking time to build allowed my planning process to mature. I was able to get to know the land and determine exactly where and how I wanted to build the house. I was particularly inspired by two books by Sarah Susanka,[18] both of which focus on building and living better, not bigger.

- I was able to hand-mill timber from the property to create a small and uniquely welcoming structure that blends beautifully with the surrounding landscape.

- The extra time allowed me to get to know my neighbors, the workings of the island's local community and suppliers, and the most streamlined and cost-effective pathways to successfully complete a project like this.

- Piece by piece, I was able to create a wonderful retreat environment for others to come to that allows them to experience the natural beauty of the Pacific Northwest while they reconnect with their own inner nature. It gives me great pleasure be with people as they experience the property when they arrive for the first time.

---

[18] Architect Sarah Susanka is the author of several books on the "not so big" way of living. In his story within this chapter, Steve refers to two of her books: *Creating the Not So Big House: Insights and Ideas for the New American Home* (Newtown, CT: Taunton Press, 2002) and *The Not So Big Life: Making Room for What Really Matters* (Newtown, CT: Taunton Press, 2007).

- Last but not least, by creating a special savings account for my dream home and waiting all those years to fulfill the dream, I was able to pay for it in full without incurring any debt.

# Exercise 2 –
# On becoming a more conscious consumer

*Affluenza*, the PBS television special mentioned earlier in the chapter, offered some great advice on evaluating and modifying spending habits that is just as valid today as it was in the late 1990s when it first aired. You can visit their website[19] to learn their ideas and techniques.

The following are a few of their tips that really stood out for us.

### Before you buy it, ask yourself
- Do I need it?
- What is the cost to have and to maintain this item?
- Could I instead borrow from or share a purchase with a friend, neighbor, or family member?
- Is there anything I already own that I could substitute for it?
- How many hours will I have to work to pay for it?

### Splurge consciously
- A few luxuries can be delightful, and they don't have to be expensive.

---

[19] These tips, questions, affirmations can be found on their website (http://affluenza.org/), where they also present additional ideas and techniques.

### Keeping up

- Pretend the Joneses are the thriftiest, least wasteful people on the block...
- Then try to keep up with them!

# Questions for reflection

- Consider how the economic downturn has affected your priorities and spending habits. Have you found yourself spending less?
- Would you say you are thinking more carefully about where and how you spend your money?
- If you have made adjustments to the amount and type of spending you usually engage in, is this because you've *had to*, based on your financial circumstances, or because you see advantages in making these changes? Either way, how does it feel to be doing things in this new way?
- What do you think about the research findings showing that our sense of life satisfaction and happiness are highest when we have our basic needs met and that having more than this can actually lead to *less* overall happiness? Does this apply in your own life? How?
- How do you determine how much is *enough* in your life? Is this something you think about and discuss with friends and family members? Would it make a difference to do so?
- If you have made significant changes lately in your approach to spending and saving, do you see yourself maintaining these changes into the future?
- If not, why?
- If so, what motivates you to continue?
- How confident are you that you will be successful?

- What do you see as the challenges that might confront you as you attempt to maintain your new checks and balances?
- What specific strategies and commitments do you need to put in place to assure your success?

## Affirmations

- I am becoming a more conscientious consumer, giving myself permission to spend less and reflect more on the purchases I make.
- I am becoming more aware of the many personal and cultural forces at play within and around me that encourage me to spend money "the way everyone else does" and give the impression that debt and money problems are normal. I choose to spend wisely and spend less.
- I appreciate what I already have in my life and embrace the concept of having enough.
- My goal is to buy things only when I need them and can afford them.
- By living within my means, I'm enjoying more of the good things that life has to offer.
- As I continue to discover my true worth and my values, I trust that there is—and will continue to be—*enough* for me to have a good life.
- As I begin to experience material abundance, I open myself to experience an abundant state of mind.

## Notes to myself _____

_____

_____

_____

_____

_____

_____

_____

_____

_____

_____

_____

_____

_____

_____

_____

_____

_____

_____

_____

_____

_____

_____

_____

_____

# Taking Stock and Clearing Out the Clutter

## Making Room for the Things That Really Matter

Three rules of work:
Out of clutter find simplicity;
From discord find harmony;
In the middle of difficulty lies opportunity.

ALBERT EINSTEIN

The best way out is always through.

ROBERT FROST

We must be the change we wish to see in the world.

MAHATMA GANDHI

I f you look up the word "clutter" in a dictionary, you'll find a combination of meanings. Some of the key ideas are: being full (too many things); disorderliness (things being out of order); confusion (things obscuring clear thinking); or noise disturbance (things making unpleasant sounds).

Typically, we think of clutter in terms of being surrounded by an excess of material stuff. If we have too much stuff, or if we haven't been taking care of our stuff, it gets in our way. We can't get things done or can't get down to doing what we really want to do because our stuff is tripping us up. All this clutter becomes burdensome in that it weighs on us. It doesn't go away and doesn't seem to de-clutter itself on its own! To make space for finding more of the Upside in your life, however, we're asking you to open yourself to thinking about clutter in broader terms than just material stuff.

## Clutter on many levels

We're defining clutter as anything in one's physical environment (*external clutter*) as well as anything in our mind, body, heart, or relationships (*internal clutter*) that interferes with our ability to think, feel, speak, or act with clarity. Clutter also comes into play when we hang on to things that served us well at one point in our lives but are no longer relevant or useful to us.

In a way, clutter is like energy: when it piles up and we can't use it well, it becomes wasted energy.

Let's face it: we'll never be rid of clutter. Internally and externally, as we move through our days there will always be things piling up to some degree. It's a fact of life, a part of the constant change that is inherent in living. The extent to which we allow things to pile up, on the outside and on the inside, determines our degree of freedom and flexibility to meet life as it comes.

Not everyone has the same tolerance for clutter: some of us can handle a lot of it and still seem to be fairly effective in managing our lives well, whereas others are thrown into a state of stress and even ill health when their environments or their relationships become burdened with unresolved issues.

We often don't realize the impact that even a small amount of clutter can have until its hold on us is released. Recall a time, for example, when you cleaned out a closet or your garage or tackled a messy desktop. You finished the job and paused to enjoy the fruits of your labor. You felt exhilarated and, in the back of your mind, wondered why it took you so long to finally get around to doing something that feels this good when it's done. You promise yourself that next time you'll get to it *much* sooner, even though you know you probably won't—and that's another aspect of the mysterious relationship we have with clutter.

## Reducing clutter: an exercise in "weight-lifting"

To create more space in your life for finding the Upside, we're inviting you to take a sincere and searching look at how cluttered your life is at this point and what steps you might take to reduce it. By lightening your load internally and externally, you'll have more energy and resources available to meet your life as it is and create more of what you want.

Both external and internal clutter can have a similar effect on our insides: a feeling of being weighted down by something that prevents or limits us from moving forward in life. Whatever form it takes, clutter creates weight that presses down on us: piles of paper on a desk; boxes of stuff in a living room or closet; beliefs that limit us or self-talk that impedes our capacity for positive thinking and actions; conversations in our head where we keep playing out unresolved arguments and conflicts; or a schedule of obligations so full that there's no room to breathe—or scream! We can't move or think clearly.

Julie Morgenstern, in her book *When Organizing Isn't Enough: SHED Your Stuff, Change Your Life,*[20] drives home the point that organizing and time-management skills aren't enough, especially when our lives are in a period of flux. According to Morgenstern, in order to be proactive in managing a time of transition and the accompanying feelings of being stuck or unsure about the future, we need to release burdensome objects and obligations to create the space to discover what's next. This freeing-up process helps us gather the energy and courage needed to move forward. Her approach, however, isn't just about de-cluttering to simplify life. It's about making the most of an opportunity for self-discovery and healthy growth through *learning about your attachment to the clutter before you let it go.*

The Upside to Morgenstern's approach is that it's about a new way of being that generates movement and fuels transformation. If you're ready to begin such a process, Morgenstern has created a helpful website filled with a variety of mini-assessments, clutter reduction videos, and worksheets for managing stuff, time, finances, and priorities more effectively: http://www.juliemorgenstern.com/LearningTools/Surveys/

## Internal clutter: the complex landscape of our mental and emotional states

We're all familiar with the folk wisdom idea that positive emotions are good for our health, contributing to our psychological and physical well-being in the form of more effective coping. In Chapter

---

[20] Julie Morgenstern, When Organizing Isn't Enough: SHED Your Stuff, Change Your Life (New York: Fireside Books, 2008). Also see: http://www.juliemorgenstern.com/LearningTools/Surveys/

One, we looked at the concept of psychological resilience and some of the research showing that positive emotions serve a buffering function and provide a useful antidote to the problems associated with negative emotions and ill health.

Maintaining positive emotional states during challenging times, however, is not an easy task to accomplish. Even when we know that to do so will make a significant difference in our capacity to adjust, heal, problem-solve, and become more resourceful in all areas of life, it's not that simple to keep our negative emotions in check and our positive thinking on track.

A common experience in difficult periods in our lives is one where time—the experience of the flow or progression as we move through each day—seems to slow down dramatically. During these experiences, not only do we come face to face with the arduous situation at hand but are also often confronted with surprising new information about ourselves, and sometimes even a detailed glimpse of our life story as a whole. In the extreme, we may (sometimes painfully) watch our entire life to date pass before us, frame by frame.

While this can stir up plenty of emotions, such periods of internal upheaval and reflection can also—if we're open to working with the content—lead us to a more realistic perspective about ourselves, allowing us to realign our focus to what is authentically most important to us.

Elliot Aronson, author of many popular books on social psychology and recognized as one of the top hundred psychologists of the twentieth century,[21] has written extensively on how we struggle when we are faced with new and uncharacteristic information about

---

[21] On Elliot Aronson's prominence in the field of social psychology, see Steven Haggbloom, "100 Most Eminent Psychologists in the 20th Century," Review of General Psychology, Vol. 6, No. 2 (2002), pp. 139-52.

ourselves.[22] Aronson was a student in the 1950s of Leon Festinger, the man who coined the term "cognitive dissonance" and expanded public knowledge about this now widely accepted and researched concept in social psychology.

Cognitive dissonance theory is broadly defined as the process human beings go through to resolve the discomfort we feel when we experience conflicting information in our attitudes, beliefs, behaviors, or emotional states. In short, when we think and act in ways that are consistent and familiar to us, we are in a harmonious state. However, when we are faced with two contradictory ideas about ourselves at the same time, cognitive dissonance theory proposes that we dislike the experience of such discrepancies so much that we will attempt to change our thinking and attitudes and/or rationalize or justify our behavior to reduce our discomfort (dissonance).

The impact on us during this brief period of internal struggle is, according to research, significant. When the experience of cognitive dissonance occurs, the reasoning areas of the brain virtually shut down. Once a justification of some kind is made and the dissonance is reduced, the emotional centers of the brain light up again.[23] We literally scramble to make some sense of ourselves in the difficult situation, and once we do—even if we end up thinking or doing something highly unusual—we begin to feel better and can function again.

---

[22] Elliot Aronson's ideas in this chapter are set out in the book he co-wrote with Carol Tavris: *Mistakes Were Made (But Not by Me): Why We Justify Foolish Beliefs, Bad Decisions, and Hurtful Acts* (Boston: Houghton Mifflin Harcourt, 2007).

[23] Psychologist Drew Westen, author of *The Political Brain: The Role of Emotion in Deciding the Fate of the Nation* (New York: Public Affairs, 2008), has done neurological research on cognitive dissonance and found that when it occurs, the reasoning areas of the brain virtually shut down. But once a justification is made, the dissonance is reduced, and the emotional centers of the brain light up "like fireworks."

# Learning from our mistakes

Aronson believes that our tendency to rationalize such conflicting beliefs in small-scale situations is a good thing because it allows us to feel better and get on with our lives, but applying this same approach to our more serious blunders creates problems in the long run. While we may temporarily feel better when we reduce the dissonance we're experiencing (for example, through excusing or justifying our actions), we aren't necessarily admitting our mistakes or learning from them. He also states that by ignoring the deeper issues, we're more apt to make the same mistakes in the future.

The best way to break out of this pattern, he says, is to become more aware of when we're in the midst of making these kinds of justifications or rationalizations. When we feel the friction of cognitive dissonance going on inside, we need to pause long enough to take a close look at what we're doing or saying to ourselves. By engaging in a closer examination of the details, we can acknowledge our mistakes, accept them as best we're able, and learn from them by making more informed decisions in the future.

The current challenges in our economy have hit all of us to some extent and many of us to a great extent. Our present situation is rife with opportunities to feel bad about mistakes we've made or to feel justified in blaming others for the circumstances we find ourselves in. Looking to the Upside in light of the research of Aronson and others, this is also an opportune time to pause and think through the details of the steps and decisions we've made that have brought us to this point, personally and collectively. Everyone makes mistakes! By resolving to learn from them rather than burying them in a knee-jerk effort to feel better temporarily, we set the stage for reducing personal clutter and making wiser choices down the road.

# Trust your biology

In a July 2007 interview on National Public Radio, Eliot Aronson pointed out an additional factor that he feels is essential to remember in challenging times: that humans, as a species, are survivors.[24] The monumental challenges we are faced with, he says, can sometimes feel bigger than life itself. His considered opinion is that at the cellular level, our deep-rooted instinct to survive is almost always stronger than the challenges life presents us with. In other words, we could benefit from a little more trust in our biology and thereby in our inherent ability to weather the storm and creatively seek out the resources and support we need to make it through the current circumstances. Reminding ourselves and others of this strength is a powerful and inspirational Upside message.

Aronson's idea seems to be supported by recent research from the University of Michigan Institute for Social Research. In a study published in September 2009 in the *Proceedings of the National Academy of Sciences*, the findings show that during major economic downturns, including the Great Depression, the average life expectancy in the United States actually increased.[25] As we know, times were tough during that particular period in U.S. history. In the stock market crash of 1929 and through the early 1930s, economic activity fell sharply (dropping 14 percent in 1932 alone) while unemployment rates soared (reaching 22.9 percent that same year).

---

[24] "Cognitive Dissonance: The Engine of Self-justification," interview with Elliot Aronson and excerpt from *Mistakes Were Made (But Not by Me)*, National Public Radio, 20 July 2007: http://www.npr.org/templates/story/story.php?storyId=12125926

[25] The research findings on life expectancy during the Great Depression can be found in the September 28, 2009, online edition of the *Proceedings of the National Academy of Sciences*: "Life and Death during the Great Depression," PNAS 2009 106:17290-17295; see http://www.pnas.org/content/106/41/17290.full?sid=7afe1001-a60b-4328-8629-f969a08808fa

Yet when researchers looked at the mortality rates among men, women, and children from 1920 to 1940, they found a surprising trend: the death rates *declined* during years of falling economic activity and rose when times were better. During the two decades spanning the 1920s and 1930s, in fact, overall life expectancy increased by 8.8 years and followed a pattern that went in the opposite direction than the rise and fall of economic activity.

As lead researcher Jose Tapia Granados reported, most people assume that periods of high unemployment are harmful to health—but, he added, this does not seem to be true.

What could this research be telling us? If we were to view old black-and-white film footage taken during the Great Depression—scenes showing people out of work or waiting for handouts in bread lines—we would be more likely to see evidence of pain and struggle than images reflecting robust health and well-being. Yet something seems to be going on during challenging times that motivates us to dig in, persevere, and even live longer on average than we do in easier times.

Perhaps, as suggested by Aronson, once we recover from the initial shock of difficult circumstances, we are biologically predisposed to access the internal resources needed to survive and even to thrive. Even though the situations we sometimes face are immensely challenging, we seem to have the ability to summon the internal fortitude to remind ourselves that we can make it through this period of adversity, whatever it takes.

Returning to more modern times and the impact of the recent economic crisis, it is vitally important to do our best to cultivate healthy emotional and mental states. We can easily dwell on the past—especially if we had a better financial balance sheet—lamenting over what we had, what we've lost, or how our life has changed for the worse. By the same token, we could fixate on a perceived negative future where we see ourselves poor and unhappy, never being able to retire, and held back from living out our dreams.

Clutter in the form of limiting thoughts and beliefs about self and the situation at hand can have a stranglehold on us, increasing the intensity of the downside of our experience and making it more difficult to find a way out the quagmire. Opening ourselves to the potential for an Upside perspective each day, as well as finding a workable routine to reduce the clutter that gets in the way, will help us put aside our more limited thinking so that our human biology— the deeper, wiser, physical and spiritual aspects of our nature—can take the lead and find the way through.

---

### Steve's story:
### "Identifying and reducing relationship clutter"

I've learned through experience that holding on to unresolved situations with others can weigh me down and dominate my thoughts and feelings. Many years ago I took a course that really piqued my interest in the deeper dynamics that occur in significant relationships. In doing the coursework required, I realized that even with my ongoing efforts to live as much as possible in right relationship with others, a fair amount of my internal space was being occupied by "relationship clutter." I decided I needed to work through the unfinished business I was carrying and commit myself to keeping future relationships clutter-free.

This deeply personal task required a good degree of initial effort and sometimes discomfort on my part. I had to take a sincere and searching look at what was holding my attention with these individuals and the content of my underlying beliefs about them and myself. Over time, I found the most appropriate way to come to terms with each person on my list, communicating when appropriate as best I could, and letting go of the rest.

I was surprised at the depth of the emotional charge I had been carrying with one or two of these individuals. But I was more surprised by the powerful effects I personally experienced as a result of doing this work. I felt freer, lighter, and more appreciative of my positive traits. Instead of being immersed in constantly reliving the situation and beating up myself and/or the other person, I actually felt more tolerant of myself as a loving, caring, human being. By loving myself and letting the grievances go, I lightened my load.

The payoffs have certainly been worth the effort. These days, I'm much better at recognizing the ways I can unintentionally add homework to my emotional in-box. With practice and intention, I find it easier to apologize when I have been in error. I also find myself able to let go of issues or grievances once I truly feel that I've done what I can on my end of the situation. I've learned that letting go not only helps to keep my relationships "clean" but also leaves all sorts of room for me to experience and enjoy the true present in my relationships and daily activities. When I keep up my regular practice of letting go, there is more of me present to participate and enjoy whatever it is I'm doing.

I've also learned a good deal about forgiveness, which is a powerful form of letting go. When I look carefully at the content of any relationship clutter I'm experiencing, I can usually find some aspect of the other person's behavior, or my own, that I wish were different. By reminding myself that I can't change the past or change other people, I can loosen my grip on the experience and determine if action or communication is needed in the present to reduce my internal clutter. Beyond this, the best thing I can do for others and myself is to forgive and move on.

Hand-in-hand with forgiveness is patience. Believe me, it's been tough work for me to become more accepting and patient of things as they are! By nature I am not a patient person. A born New Yorker, I inherited the New-York-minute state of mind, and even though I left the Big Apple thirty-five years ago and now live on a tiny laid-back island of eight hundred people, I still carry this trait and likely will for the rest of my life. The good news is that I'm keenly aware of this pattern, and I work daily at reducing its impact on others and myself.

One last important component in my strategy for keeping my internal clutter to a minimum is an intention to surround myself with positive, supportive people. I seek out and cultivate relationships with others who are similarly interested in meaningful interactions and who are willing to engage in a process of working through challenging dynamics when they occur. Even if we don't agree on an issue, or if one of us is clumsy in the attempt to explain our position, there's room for human error and giving each other the benefit of the doubt as we fumble our way toward a place of resolution. This kind of mutual support in my core relationships helps me to maintain and enhance my personal strengths and primes me to be more fully available for others.

## Never underestimate the power of forgiveness

Forgiveness is one of those words that are hard to describe, even though each of us has a fairly clear idea of what it means. When we experience hurt at the words or actions of others, a range of feelings can result: anger, disappointment, bitterness, sadness, and resentment. Our human tendency is to internalize these emotional wounds, giving them power over us and detracting from our ability to enjoy the present. The resulting stuck feelings can, like a pair of corrective lenses, alter our perception of the people and the world around us and distort our experiences. Without realizing it, we may be bringing our unresolved hurts into every relationship and new experience.

When we enter into a process of forgiveness, however, we eventually untangle ourselves from the thoughts and feelings that keep us tied to these painful events. By forgiving, we release our hold on the past and the actions of other people—and *their* hold on us.

The most powerful thing to remember about forgiveness is that it isn't something we do for others; it's a step we take for ourselves so we can let go of the negative emotional baggage we carry. According to Dr. Katherine M. Piderman of the Mayo Clinic's Adult Health department, research shows that holding onto grudges and bitterness results in long-term health problems. Conversely, research is now revealing that forgiveness offers many health benefits,[26] including:

- Lower blood pressure
- Stress reduction
- Less hostility
- Better anger-management skills
- Lower heart rate
- Lower risk of alcohol or substance abuse
- Fewer depression symptoms
- Fewer anxiety symptoms

---

[26] Mayo Clinic staff members contribute to articles found on the Mayo Clinic online health website. See the article on forgiveness by Dr. Katherine M. Piderman at: http://www.mayoclinic.com/health/forgiveness/MH00131

- Reduction in chronic pain
- More friendships
- Healthier relationships
- Greater religious or spiritual well-being
- Improved psychological well-being

Dr. Piderman points out, in that same online article about forgiveness, that forgiving isn't the same thing as forgetting: "The act that hurt or offended you may always remain a part of your life. But forgiveness can lessen its grip on you and help you focus on other, positive parts of your life. Forgiveness also doesn't mean that you deny the other person's responsibility for hurting you, and it doesn't minimize or justify the wrong. You can forgive the person without excusing the act." In the words of Buddhist monk Jack Kornfield, author and teacher: "Forgiveness is primarily for our own sake, so that we no longer carry the burden of resentment. But to forgive does not mean we will allow injustice again."[27]

Frederic Luskin, Ph.D., Director of the Stanford Forgiveness Projects, offers training in forgiveness through a program titled *Forgive For Good*, which has been consistently validated by research at Stanford University. His work confirms the benefits of the practice of forgiveness for psychological, relationship, and physical health.[28] Dr. Luskin has explored forgiveness therapy with people still suffering from the violence in Northern Ireland, Sierra Leone, and the 9/11 attacks on the World Trade Center, as well as with individuals in corporate, medical, legal, and religious settings. When we forgive others

---

[27] Kornfield is quoted, among other places, in his blog entry of 8 July 2009, "Should a Buddhist ever resort to violence?" on the website *Progressive Buddhism*: http://progressivebuddhism.blogspot.com/2009/07/should-buddhist-ever-resort-to-violence.html

[28] Frederic Luskin is Director of the Stanford Forgiveness Projects. His work is featured on his website *Forgive for Good*: http://www.learningtoforgive.com/

who have hurt or wronged us, according to Luskin, we experience greater feelings of optimism, hope, compassion, and self-confidence.

Confucius says the more we know ourselves, the more we forgive ourselves. If we're looking to experience more of the Upside in challenging times, forgiveness is something we need to take seriously as an essential tool for de-cluttering our internal space, building resilience, and improving our overall sense of well-being.

## Getting to work on personal clutter

As we knuckle down and get to work on reducing external and internal clutter in our lives, we create more space and freedom to be fully available for whatever life brings to us. This enhanced ability to be *responsive* rather than *reactive* supports us in bringing our best self forward to meet each person and situation along our path.

As with forgiveness, there is no one best way to begin to assess and deal with the clutter in your life. Curiosity and an open mind are excellent places to begin. In the next chapter, we'll explore the concept of synchronicity and the ever-present availability of small sparks of insight and inspiration to guide your unique journey. The important thing here is not *how* you get started, but that you *do*!

---

### Barbara's story:
### "Early influences and the link
### between internal and external clutter"

I grew up learning to protect my space and my belongings. The second oldest of five children in a middle-class, blue-collar family, I shared a ten-by-twelve-foot bedroom with my two sisters. The space was informally divided by handmade bunk beds on one side of the room and my older sister's single bed on the other. Our chest of drawers was divided into three equal sections, with two larger and one smaller drawer apiece. The closet was also divided into three: one-third each for clothing, shoes, and whatever else we possessed.

This living arrangement continued right up until my older sister reached her later teenage years, when my father built a makeshift bedroom in a corner of the basement rec room. She moved downstairs and my younger sister and I graduated to twin beds, three large drawers each and half of the closet space. The contrast was luxurious!

I internalized a few not-so-helpful tendencies from the cramped environment of my childhood years: I guard my personal stuff; I crave space to spread out into; and if there is too much disorder in my physical environment, I can quickly feel cluttered and imbalanced on the inside. I also have a tendency to hang onto things longer than necessary and then to start rationalizing why this is actually a good and practical idea. But I've learned my deepest lessons about clutter through observing and interacting with others in my adult years.

## Clutter is a personal matter until we have to get along with other people

The way I see it, the amount of material stuff we have in our lives is relative: what might seem like excess to me may in fact seem like not much to someone else. Based on the amount of space we live in, our capacity to organize and take care of possessions, and our degree of satisfaction with what we have, I believe that each of us can find some degree of balance through peacefully co-existing with our stuff. It's the *co-existing with others* that ushers in the challenges.

For example, I don't take kindly to someone else referring to my prized possessions as clutter (translation: "junk"), and by the same token, I'm not all that fond of putting up with another's *unreasonable* amount of *useless stuff* (translation: more junk than I have). Plus, if I have to tolerate other people's clutter in ways I don't like, I can end up feeling irritated or resentful, which interferes with my good feelings toward them. It's easy to see how the trouble starts.

What works for me, after many decades of ups and downs in my progress along the path of figuring out how much is *enough*, are regular reviews. The thing I've come to learn about stuff is this: if we don't see it, and if we don't regularly review it to know how we still feel about it, it tends to become a permanent resident. This is true in dealing with both external clutter (material things) and internal issues (the known and unknown clutter I carry around within me about myself and those I'm in relationship with).

**Keeping the lid on external clutter.** To avoid external build-up to the point of clutter, I regularly sort through my belongings in their respective resting places: closets, drawers, storage bins, cupboards, and even the garage. I make a point of going through pretty much everything in the house (that is, everything in the "mine" and "ours" categories, since I don't transgress into my spouse's personal stuff) to see how I feel about it. I do only a limited amount at a time to avoid being overwhelmed. And I do this type of task only on days when I'm feeling emotionally centered and readily able to part with things that are not essential.

If an item is no longer needed or wanted, I take it wherever it needs to go so that someone else—a community charity or recycling source, for example—can use it. If shared ownership or attachment is involved, I'll consult with the other party to reach a mutual decision. If the item is to be kept, I store it or place it in whatever way now seems appropriate. If an item falls into a gray zone, meaning that I'm not sure I still want or need it but am also not quite ready to part with it, I hang onto it—but now it has a sort of invisible bookmark on it. Its days are now numbered, since I've come to know from experience I'm getting ready to part with it. Either someone else will soon need it, or it won't make it through the next round of review.

There are many upsides to this ongoing material stuff-management system for me: I keep current with what and how much I actually have; I often have the joyful experience of having just the right thing to give away at the right time to someone who needs it; I feel lighter inside when I know my "house is in order"; and my ability to think clearly and meet each day with flexibility is noticeably improved when I look around me and am sure there are no major unknown stashes of goods lurking in dark corners needing attention.

**Easing the burden of internal clutter.** Similarly, to avoid internal build-up of mental and emotional clutter, I follow a fluid pattern of regular review that includes:

- **Daily outdoor walks** at an exercise pace. The movement of my body and the backdrop of nature seem to sort through the various strands of thoughts seeking my attention on any particular day. I don't take an MP3 device along with me when walking because, for me, the noise and information just seems to *add* to my mental stuff rather than release it.

- **Moments to pause and reflect**, whenever I feel a nagging sense of something being not quite right. I've learned to take notice when I'm feeling preoccupied. I simply focus my attention and do a brief scan of my current thoughts and feelings so I can pin down the issue that's disturbing me and define it in words—for instance, "It's bugging me that I haven't heard from my parents in a few days. I'd better give them a call."

While I'm not always ready or able to take immediate action on whatever it is, just the act of identifying it helps release its hold over my mental space. If I do feel it's appropriate and beneficial to communicate with someone about an issue, I first think through the best way to approach it—in person, on the phone, or in writing via a letter or email message—and then I either let it go, knowing I'll find the opportune time to follow through, or take the needed action.

- **Finding time for daily mindfulness meditation.** I aim to make time each day to practice seated meditation, for fifteen minutes or longer, to tune into my breathing and physical body and to gradually let go of my thinking mind and my attachment to all its various content.

- **Reading an inspirational book** for a few minutes before going to sleep each night. This helps me release the contents of the day and shift into an expansive state of mind that promotes self-acceptance, peacefulness, and a sense of gratitude for the complicated and wonderful experience of being a spiritual being in a human body.

- **Brief morning reflections on my dreams** upon awakening. I regularly write down my night dreams in a bedside notebook to help me acknowledge the wisdom of the unconscious mind and to learn what I can from its symbolic gifts.

## Wisdom to know the difference

I'm coming to terms with the fact that I can truly be responsible for attending only to my own clutter, whether it's on the inside—in my thoughts and feelings about myself and others—or in the material realm of my personal space or the world around me. Thanks to one beloved member of my family and her path with addictions, I've developed an intimate relationship with the first verse of the Serenity Prayer: "God grant me the serenity to accept the things I cannot change; courage to change the things I can; and wisdom to know the difference." Whenever an issue is troubling me, I can always return to this vast and wonderful sentence and eventually find my way to figuring out what, if anything, I can or need to change. It's a source of inspiration that helps me to cut through the clutter, get back on track, and remain open for the things in life that really matter to me.

## Exercise 3 - A place to begin: how's *your* relationship with clutter?

The following four questions are simple sliding scales to jumpstart your personal assessment of the degree of clutter in your life, including the type(s) of clutter that might need your attention first. For each question, read the five descriptive statements and determine which one best fits (a) your current status with respect to the type of clutter being described, and (b) the relationship you would prefer to have with this type of clutter. Write the number for the statement you've selected (1 through 5) in the space beside both the "Current" and "Preferred" indicators. The degree to which your answers for (a) and (b) are distant from each other (that is, where you are now versus where you'd optimally like to be in your life) reveals the amount of work you have to do with respect to resolving issues about clutter.

1(a) Which statements best describe your current and preferred state regarding physical clutter (material stuff) in your life?

Physical Clutter         __ Current __ Preferred

  1. My living and work spaces are cluttered and unsatisfactory.

  2. I'm somewhere in between (1) and (3).

  3. My living and work spaces are sometimes organized to my satisfaction.

  4. I'm somewhere in between (3) and (5).

  5. My living and work spaces are usually organized to my satisfaction.

1(b) If there is a gap between your current and preferred states, what specific actions are you prepared to take at this time?

_____

_____

_____

_____

2(a) Which statements best describe your current and preferred states regarding mental clutter (the insistent, often negative, thoughts that clutter your thinking):

Mental Clutter         __ Current __ Preferred

  1. Negative thoughts usually dominate my thinking.

  2. I'm somewhere in between (1) and (3).

3. I am conscious of my negative thoughts and want to be more positive.

4. I'm somewhere in between (3) and (5).

5. Positive thoughts dominate my thinking most of the time.

2(b) If there is a gap between your current and preferred states, what specific actions are you prepared to take at this time?

_____

_____

_____

_____

_____

3(a) Which statements best describe your current and pre-ferred states regarding emotional clutter (unresolved feelings and emotions that get in the way of fully expe-riencing the present):

Emotional Clutter            __ Current __ Preferred

1. I am easily triggered and become outwardly reactive or withdrawn.

2. I'm somewhere in between (1) and (3).

3. I am sometimes triggered and become outwardly reac-tive or withdrawn.

4. I'm somewhere in between (3) and (5).

5. I am able to be responsive rather than outwardly reac-tive or withdrawn.

3(b) If there is a gap between your current and preferred states, what specific actions are you prepared to take at this time?

_____

_____

_____

_____

_____

4(a) Which statements best describe your current and preferred states regarding relationship clutter (carrying unresolved hurts, anger, or resentments about others):

Relationship Clutter ____ Current ____ Preferred

1. I have a number of relationships that are incomplete, and I carry emotional baggage about these.
2. I'm somewhere in between (1) and (3).
3. I am complete and at peace with some of my relationships.
4. I'm somewhere in between (3) and (5).
5. I am complete and at peace with all of my relationships.

4(b) If there is a gap between your current and preferred states, what specific actions are you prepared to take at this time?

_____

_____

_____

_____

_____

When you've completed this exercise, you can get started with the actions you're ready to take now, or you can consult the Further Resources section at the back of this book, and the accompanying website, for suggestions on how to keep developing your plan.

## Learning to pause and reflect as an aid to reducing internal clutter

The following exercise is a brief and simple way to use the ever-present gift of your breathing as a way to slow the mind, still the body, and shift to a more attentive and aware focus of the here and now, the present moment. As Albert Einstein said: "No problem can be solved from the same level of consciousness that created it." By regularly doing this meditative exercise and others like it, we can eventually train ourselves to release the grip of various stressors that inhabit our minds and bodies, allowing ourselves to gain an internal sense of clarity, focus, and calm. It takes only moments and the de-cluttering effects can be profound.

## Exercise 4 – Taking a time-out for present moment awareness

Read through these instructions first to acquaint yourself with the steps. If you like, you can record the steps into an audio playback device, leaving adequate pauses between each step, or you can take turns slowly reading through the steps with a partner.

To begin, find a time and a place where you will have as little as five and as many as fifteen to twenty minutes of uninterrupted time. Turn off the phone and any other potentially distracting devices.

If you have only a certain amount of time or don't want to be distracted by thoughts about ending on time, you might want to set a gentle-sounding timer (one without a harsh signal that might startle you) for the amount of time you have set aside.

Locate a suitable surface to sit on comfortably, such as a chair or a mat or pillow on the floor. Do your best to keep your spine in an upright position and use whatever supports you need to help your legs and back accomplish this. You might want to place a light blanket or sweater over your shoulders, because the body tends to cool down slightly when it enters a more restful state. Follow the steps below, and prepare to relax and enjoy...

- Once seated, take a moment to scan the entire length of your body and make any small adjustments in your position to make yourself more comfortable. Close your eyes, or let your gaze softly rest on a point on the floor a few feet in front of you. Take a deep breath—all the way to the bottom of your lungs—and let out a big, slow, audible sigh: "AAAhhhhhhhhhhhhhhhh...."

- Become aware of your breathing. There is nothing you need to do to adjust your breath, no need to make it faster or slower, deeper or shallower. Just *notice* the breath as it enters and leaves your body. Become aware of the sensations of the breath moving in your body. Notice where you feel this movement.

- Become aware of the area around your heart. Again, there's no need to *do* anything to this area of your body. Just allow your focus to rest here and notice the qualities of this area of your body. Waves of breath continue to enter and leave your body. Let them come and go.

- Notice that you are beginning to feel more and more relaxed.

- You may have observed that your mind continues to generate thoughts while you sit here. That's what the mind does. Become aware that there is another part of you, separate from your thoughts, that notices these thoughts and their various contents. *Take a moment to acknowledge that you are not your thoughts.* Imagine that your thoughts are like individual clouds, floating along in a blue sky. Bring your awareness to the blue sky, the vast backdrop of your spacious inner mind, and let these thought-clouds pass on by without paying attention to their details. When you find your focus moving away from the sky to follow any one cloud, just bring your attention back to the spacious blue sky. Nowhere else to be. Nothing else to do. Just be here, now.

■ Continue to allow any thoughts of *past* seconds, minutes, hours, and days in your life to float on by as you continue to rest more fully in this state of present moment time.

■ Allow any thoughts of *future* seconds, minutes, hours, and days in your life to float on by as you continue to remain aware of the gentle pattern of your breath.

■ Just rest in this peaceful place of the present moment, which is always here for us when we set aside the time and space to experience it.

■ Continue to let yourself be here, noticing the breath and allowing yourself to experience the quiet vastness of the present moment. When it's time for you to bring this experience to a close, slowly begin to allow your attention to return to your body and to your location in the room. Allowing your eyes to remain closed or gently open, as you prefer, lightly move your fingers and toes. Giving yourself another moment or two to keep your attention focused inwards, gently move and stretch your body in whatever way feels good to you. Give yourself thanks for taking this time out from your busy day to experience present moment awareness.

## Applying the benefits of present moment awareness to assist you in clearing clutter

Taking a few moments each day, whenever it's possible or needed, to relax into present moment awareness will gradually shift the way you experience and interact with yourself and the world around you. Inner calm, focused awareness, and the ability to *respond* rather than *react* to situations are not anything that others can give us. We have to learn to cultivate these gifts for ourselves.

As long as we continue to believe that someone or something outside ourselves will bring us peace, we won't experience it.

We can make use of the more peaceful and relaxed place we arrive at through the practice of present moment awareness to help us clarify the situations and relationships that need our attention. Below are some exploratory questions to stimulate insights and identify actions that can help you reduce the internal and external clutter in your life.

Try setting aside some extra time following your seated present moment awareness practice. As you bring your session to a close and begin to return your focus to the room, allow yourself to remain connected to your sense of present moment awareness as you bring to mind a person or situation that is causing you distress.

Take a few moments to gently ask yourself these or other related questions that make sense to you. You may want to keep a pen and notebook beside you as you do this so that you can jot down any new ideas or further questions that come to mind.

Try to keep yourself rooted in the deep blue sky of your deeper awareness as you reflect on the situation. If you get caught up in some of the familiar thought-clouds about the person or situation, which are usually hooked in at the same level as the problem itself and therefore not of much use to you in finding a new way to address the issue, you might not be available to "hear" the new ideas and insights that are trying to get your attention.

Give yourself permission to be patient. Even if you don't have the answers you were hoping for when you finish your session, you've set the stage for them to find their way to you, often when you least expect it.

## Questions for reflection

The following questions will help you identify and work with any past, present or future relationship clutter.

- What is it about this situation that is most bothersome to me?
- What, at a deeper level, am I telling myself about this person or situation? Do I *really* believe this? Or am I viewing the circumstances through a narrow and distorted lens? Am I keeping myself stuck in the *past* regarding what happened?
- If so, is there something I need to say or do to help me to release my grip on this experience—or its grip on me? How best can I do this?
- Do I find myself being apprehensive about some aspect of the *future* because of this person or situation?
- If so, how can I prepare myself to reduce my fear or anxiety? Or what do I need to do, or need to let go of, to ease my insides about this?
- Have I made a mistake I need to take responsibility for?
- Have I justified or rationalized my behavior just to make myself feel better? If so, is this really helping me to learn from my mistakes?
- Is forgiveness a factor in this situation? Am I willing to enter into a process of forgiving this person or event, thereby

benefiting my own health and well-being? If not, what remains in the way of forgiveness?

■ How can I be most helpful (caring, loving, etc.) to myself as I work through these issues?

■ Do I feel comfortable enough working through these issues on my own, or would it be helpful for me to talk with a trusted friend or therapist?

## Affirmations

■ Clutter is a familiar friend and a good teacher. As I address the various kinds of clutter in my life and take steps to reduce it, I am making space for the things that matter most to me.

■ Every day, I am making progress in my ability to think, feel, speak, and act with clarity. Meeting life fully in the present moment, my internal clutter falls away.

■ I am learning to trust my biology, knowing that at the deepest level I am powerfully made to survive and thrive, even in the midst of life's challenges.

## Notes to myself _____

# CHAPTER FOUR

# Fully Alive

## Meeting Life in the Present Moment and Making the Most of its Gifts and Challenges

People say that what we're all seeking is a meaning for life.... I think that what we're really seeking is an experience of being alive, so that our life experiences on the purely physical plane will have resonance within our innermost being and reality, so we can actually feel the rapture of being alive.

JOSEPH CAMPBELL

Don't ask yourself what the world needs;
ask yourself what makes you come alive.
And then go and do that.
Because what the world needs is people who have come alive.

HOWARD THURMAN

When a great moment knocks on the door of your life,
it is often no louder than the beating of your heart,
and it is very easy to miss it.

BORIS PASTERNAK

Difficult times can rob us of our energy and enthusiasm for life. While all of us will face challenges in the course of a lifetime, when the number or intensity of these events escalates to the point of stretching our ability to cope, it can be hard to muster up the resolve to get through the day. How then—and especially in times like these—is it possible to imagine feeling what Joseph Campbell describes as "the rapture of being alive"?

In the introduction, we mentioned clients, friends, and colleagues who reported they were finding unexpected, positive new elements in their lives *even when their circumstances seemed to be in a downward spiral.* Most of them were completely surprised by these beneficial outcomes. They didn't intentionally go looking for any silver linings in the gray clouds that engulfed them. It was more often in hindsight that they noticed one or more important aspects of their lives had improved, even in conditions of adversity.

In addition, some were able to describe a series of small, apparently coincidental events that led to new ideas to ponder or actions to take. In being willing to follow these subtle nudges—often because they were at their wits' end or operating at a slower pace than usual— they found their so-called "bad" circumstances pointing the way to previously unconsidered "good" options. Not only was it surprising to find a light at the end of the tunnel, these individuals also discovered that it wasn't located anywhere near where they might have looked had they been in their usual mode of thinking and operating.

Several also wondered whether they would ever have been able to imagine or arrive at the positive new outcomes they were experiencing *if life hadn't brought about the dire circumstances that affected them so deeply.* Perhaps there's truth to the old saying: "If you keep on thinking what you've always thought, you'll keep on getting what you've always got!"

In talking with everyday people, those who inspired us to write this book, we learned that it took time for them to begin to notice the Upsides among the challenges. In reflecting on what they were learning in their current circumstances—or what life was teaching them—they found themselves shifting long-held core values, leading to often-dramatic changes in lifestyle and their process for making important decisions.

## The Upside of hard times

While unsettling, the times in our lives when we feel least in control of the outcomes or destinations ahead may be the most fertile for growth and change. Personal crises bring us to a different state of awareness, whether these crises are financial downturns, personal challenges in health, work, and relationships, or societal events like 9/11. As we grapple with times of upheaval and attempt to make sense of them, we access powerful emotions and insights that often go unnoticed during more stable times.

During challenging times, we may be asking ourselves such questions as:

- What is most important to me?
- What brings meaning, happiness, and pleasure to my life?
- Have I been wasting time and energy in directions that don't really matter all that much to me?
- What have I always wanted to do that I never seem to get around to?
- Is there unfinished business I've been avoiding?
- What is the cost to me, personally, for continuing to put off these things?

There is something about being in the thick of difficulties that cuts through the superficial layers of existence and lands us in a grounded, somber place. While such times may not feel as good as those when there are no pressing issues capturing our attention, there are valuable qualities in us that often come forward when we're faced with problems we can't escape or deny. Some of these qualities are:

- a heightened sensitivity in our thoughts, emotions, and exchanges with others, combined with a tendency to say what we mean and mean what we say (even if we can't help this because we're more emotional and less guarded than usual);

- the motivation to take matters seriously rather than put them off, weighing options and being willing to consult with others who might be able to help us figure things out (even if we feel embarrassed to admit that we're in trouble, we know we cannot handle the situation on our own);

- a willingness to see our part in the problems we're facing and make amends as needed, instead of becoming sidetracked with defensiveness, blame, and vengefulness (even if we have to eat humble pie, we see the value in lightening our personal load by admitting when we're wrong or have otherwise missed the mark);

- a yearning for simplicity in our day-to-day life, cutting ourselves loose from extraneous activities that drain our already-taxed energies (even though it might disappoint others or trigger criticism, we see the need for self-care and give ourselves permission to slow down);

- the realization that we're not the only one hurting due to problems, that others have made it through even worse circumstances than ours (even if we're feeling self-pity about our situation, we see the limits of "Why me?" thinking and decide to channel our energies into finding a way through the adversity, instead of complaining about the way things are).

## F. E.A.R. = False Evidence Appearing Real

Granted, the line-up above is somewhat of a problem-solving wish list. If we're honest, all of us can cite numerous examples of times when we were faced with difficulties and didn't handle them very well. But if challenging times have the capacity to bring out the best in us, why do we usually end up wishing, when the going gets tough, that things were better? And what is it that gets in the way of the best in us coming forward to meet life's circumstances, preventing us from handling our difficulties with the wish-list kinds of qualities?

Most of us are familiar with the powerful emotion of fear, the feeling of distress that is aroused in us by a sense of impending danger, pain, or something bad about to happen. The aspect of fear we're not so familiar with in modern times is whether the threat is real or imagined. When we don't take the time to explore and confirm that fear is working in us, we tend to shift automatically into a defensive way of meeting others and the situations we face.

One way to simplify the experience of fear is to look at it as arising from one of two sources: the body or the mind.[29] Fear arising in the body—that is, fear generated by our physiological system, including our five senses (sight, hearing, taste, smell, touch) and our intuition—can be a very helpful indicator to keep us safe. This type of fear is an early warning system that alerts us to real danger and triggers our biology to act accordingly. When we experience this type of fear, we need to pay close attention so that we can assess the extent of the threat and be prepared to stop in our tracks (freeze) or get

---

[29] This concept of seeing fear as arising from either the body or the mind is one that Barbara Taylor internalized in this particular way, many years ago, as a result of exposure to various First Nations oral teachings. She neither takes credit for the idea nor can she attribute it to a specific source.

as far away as possible (flee). A further option that can arise is the need for some type of self-protection (fight).

The second type of fear—the kind that arises in our thoughts—is not only more insidious but is the variety of fear that is at work within us most of the time, including when we're not even aware of its presence. This type of fear is tied to thoughts of concern or anxiety. It distorts our perception and can confuse us as to what's really going on.

Such fear in the mind is self-perpetuating, in that the distorted ideas arise either from within or we hear them from others and accept them as valid. Fear-based thoughts can stir up our emotions and lead to the creation of a complex fortress of internal beliefs that can become solidly entrenched, influencing our interactions with others and narrowing our outlook on life.

Michael Singer, author of the book *The Untethered Soul: The Journey Beyond Yourself*, notes an interesting change in the evolutionary instinct to survive, one that may impact the human fear response in many cultures. "During eons of evolution, from the simplest of living forms to the most complex," he writes, "there has always been the day-to-day struggle to protect oneself. In our highly evolved cooperative social structures, this survival instinct has gone through evolutionary changes. Many of us no longer lack food, water, clothing, or shelter, nor do we regularly face life-threatening physical danger. As a result, the protective energies have adapted toward defending the individual psychologically, rather than physiologically. We now experience the daily need to defend our self-concepts rather than our bodies. Our major struggles end up being with our own inner fears, insecurities, and destructive behavior patterns, and not with outside forces."[30]

---

[30] Michael Singer, *The Untethered Soul: The Journey Beyond Yourself* (Oakland, CA: Noetic Books/New Harbinger Publications, 2007).

The net result of this shift, according to Singer, is that our psychological triggers for the fear response have become overly sensitized and out of balance. Even though situations pose no physical danger to us, we feel the need to protect ourselves as if they did. When this occurs, we close down in order to shield ourselves from the perceived threat, but by doing so, we avoid personal growth and remain stuck in our old ways.

When we take a closer look at the messages that fear whispers in our ears, we can see that this relentless string of what-if scenarios of doom and gloom are really a distorted attempt to help us identify and stave off a possibly bigger problem. When we listen closely, we can detect a familiar pattern to our beliefs and conditioned behavior patterns. The problem is that the more we listen to fear and let it influence our thinking and actions, the more we remain its prisoner. It is only in examining the bottom-line content of these internal messages that we can hold them up to scrutiny, thereby challenging their accuracy and questioning their authority about what we know to be true for our deepest self.

When we hold our distorted thinking up to the clear light of day and measure its truth and validity, we are able to detect whether it is False Evidence Appearing Real, or F. E.A.R. When we begin to see fear for what it is, including all of its accompanying demands, conditions, expectations, obligations, and irrational scenarios, we slowly begin to set ourselves free from its grip on us. Instead of bracing ourselves and closing down, we can remind ourselves to remain open and to let go of our need to control all the details. We can begin to create space for paying attention in new and creative ways to the inner, intuitive voice within, the voice that is silenced when we're in the grip of fear.

Challenging times in our lives present an open invitation for our fears to surface. If our intention is to learn and grow from our experiences, then there is no point in resisting our fears and insecurities when they arise. Rather than let them get in the way—triggering us to close down, react, and remain stuck—we can make a place at the table for our fears and start to work with them, while at the same time inviting the best in us to come forward to help find new solutions to the problems we face. As we welcome the many varieties of fear that arise within us and see those fears for what they really are, we can begin to shift our unburdened awareness to new ways of paying attention to life.

## The quality of our attention

It should be evident by now that we humans are very complex beings. Even when we're not paying full attention, we're constantly monitoring and processing the external world around us and the internal physical functions that keep our bodies alive. In addition, whether or not we're aware of it, our experience is influenced by the mental, emotional, and spiritual layers that shape us uniquely as individuals.

The basic functioning of our amazing bodies occurs without conscious direction from us. In addition, we don't usually need to give much thought to exactly how we manage many of the routine external details in our lives: how we wake up and get dressed each morning, brush our teeth, feed the cat, or even drive a car from point A to point B. We don't have to give such things much thought. We just go ahead and do them, sometimes without remembering that we did.

It's obvious that many of these learned, automatic sequences of thought and behavior are helpful to us. When we shift into autopilot mode, however, we rely on familiar ways of experiencing and inter-preting the world rather than meeting each moment with awareness and curiosity. It's only when something unusual happens, something we didn't expect, that we sit up, take notice, and become curious about what's going on.

Challenging times, then, provide us with yet another opportu-nity, if we can muster up the courage to view things this way. In such times, we can't continue to operate on autopilot. We have to inter-rupt our internal cruise-control abilities and navigate more carefully into and through the unfamiliar and tenuous situations at hand. As we work to keep our fears in check, we have the additional opportu-nity to *shift the way we pay attention to life so that we can be more fully in the present moment, where life is unfolding.*

**Real life happens here and now**—today, this very moment, followed by the next moment. When we're not fully engaged in the present moment, our thoughts tend to wander off while we ruminate about the past or speculate about the future. While we can certainly learn from the past, and though it's true we need to do at least a modicum of planning to prepare us for the future, our tendency is to spend the majority of our time in either the past or the future, miss-ing entirely the subtle wonders of the present moment. At the same time, we tend to miss the more subtle clues and signals available in the present that could lead us to new life directions and innovative solutions to the problems at hand.

By beginning to accept life the way it unfolds instead of focus-ing on the past or the future, or on how life *should* be, there will be more of you available to notice the potential opportunities right here around you, opportunities that can lead to the internal and external resources you need for whatever is next.

## Internal combustion: harnessing sparks to ignite a new way of meeting life

The basic principle of the internal combustion engines that power most cars on the road today is centered on the process of **ignition**: setting fire to fuel in a combustion cylinder. To put it simply, a car battery provides a high-voltage electrical spark that ignites the air-fuel mix in the engine's cylinders. The resulting expansion of the hot pressurized gases creates useful mechanical energy in the form of a powerful force, which is harnessed by components in the engine to move the car forward.

Metaphorically speaking, a similar process occurs within us each time an event or idea stirs our interest or stimulates our imagination. We feel ignited or sparked by what's going on around and within us. We notice a heightened degree of energy in a new direction, which we experience as interest, motivation, or an urge towards immediate action. Let's call this **the human process of internal combustion.**

It all begins with ignition, which in humans is a little less predictable than that of the mechanical process in internal combustion engines. When we engage the ignition in our cars, we expect the engine to run and to keep running until we turn it off. We humans, however, cannot always put a finger on what will motivate us or how long the inspiration will last. It's easier for many of us to figure out what we *don't* want or *don't* like than it is to determine what we *do* want in life.

Take a moment to consider a few of the most powerful events or insights that have occurred in your own life. How did these come about? Were they a result of purposeful action or research on your part? Many people typically report that such life-changing moments weren't planned but that they found themselves taken by surprise into new and unexpected territories that had a potent impact on the direction of their lives from that point forward.

The process of inspirational ignition in human beings is indeed mysterious. It is often very subtle. Unintentionally, we can miss an internal spark entirely and bypass the chance for that process of combustion within us. Instead of experiencing the internal nudge to move forward in a new or previously underdeveloped direction, we filter out the various signals we're receiving and keep on with business as usual.

In North America, we live in a culture that encourages us to keep busy and be productive. Through advertising and the societal consensus around us, we're bombarded with messages each day to pursue wholeheartedly the good life and whatever it takes to get there. We're impelled to drive ourselves ever forward in the direction of work, earning an income, and supporting the national economy through the purchase of endless goods and services.

The basic message we've internalized is this: keep your nose to the grindstone, stay out of trouble, and eventually, you'll be able to retire and relax. Sometimes it seems as if the only real break we're allowed to have to stop and smell the roses, to slow down and savor life in a sane and nourishing way, is either during our brief days of sanctioned vacation each year or when we get sick and have permission to be excused from our usual daily responsibilities. Sound familiar?

How often have you experienced authentic encouragement for attending to the more subtle clues that are available each day, pointing you toward new avenues of personal exploration? While we've all been hearing a lot more in recent years about "following your bliss," it's not quite clear how we're supposed to accomplish this. It's especially unclear how we could manage this and still be practical, contributing, self-supporting members of society.

What we're suggesting that you try is this: **begin today to pay attention to the sparks that can lead to ignition in your life.**

Sparks are occurring all the time around us and within us— whether we're paying attention or not. As mentioned earlier, each time an event or an idea stirs our interest or stimulates our imagination, we are experiencing a sort of special spark. By beginning to notice these subtle flashes and becoming curious about them, we set the stage for ignition: a heightened degree of energy in the form of a new idea, or a brand new connection that sheds insight on a problem we've been mulling over, or the illumination of a possible new direction we hadn't considered before.

When we acknowledge that life is showing us something new that's personally relevant and could even be life-changing, interest is generated that leads to motivation and action. This is the human process of internal combustion, and it all begins with a tiny, often easy-to-miss spark.

What we're also talking about here is *synchronicity*. The concept was first encapsulated by Swiss psychiatrist Carl Jung: that seemingly unrelated occurrences in daily life are actually meaningfully related according to a larger, unseen framework of wisdom and intelligence.[31] The more you look for and pay attention to synchronicities, the more interactive and dynamic your life becomes.

As we begin to sense a deeper intelligence in life, we naturally begin to take more interest in how daily sparks are always pointing to something worth paying attention to. Rather than clinging to a wish list of expectations and beliefs about how life is *supposed* to

---

[31] Carl G. Jung's ideas on synchronicity are included in his own books and expanded upon in many books written since by other Jungian authors.

be, we can step back, take a breath, and open to a sense of wonder and curiosity about life on its own terms. While we may not like some of what comes our way, we can make the choice to release the outworn reaction of struggling against it. We can orient ourselves instead to look for a deeper and more resonant response from within.

Our circumstances could always be better or worse than they are now. As we begin to let go of our familiar attempts to get what we want out of life, we can begin to accept, appreciate, and grow from what is actually happening as life unfolds. By remaining open and responsive rather than inflexible and reactive, we can authentically meet life moment by moment and make the most of it.

## Recognizing sparks amidst the clutter

In Chapter Three, we looked at the concept of clutter and the meanings that have come to be associated with the word: disorderliness, confusion, and a sense of being full to the point of overflowing. Clutter, then, is a pretty good word to describe the way we experience our thoughts and feelings from time to time.

Cluttered insides can be easier to recognize when things are on the verge of being out of control, times when we're so full on the inside that it's hard to think clearly and interact well with others. But even in quieter times, when we are busy with the usual activities of our day, there is a certain amount of unhelpful clutter going on beyond the range of our immediate awareness. This more subtle mental clutter, when left undetected, sets up an internal navigational system that filters our experience and keeps us on autopilot.

When we're in autopilot mode:

- We are not aware of the internal dialogues going on in our heads that pressure us to respond or react to situations in similar, familiar, and often limiting ways.

- We are usually occupying ourselves with thoughts that have to do with the past or the future, and we are therefore only partially available to be present with ourselves and others in the immediacy of now.

- We view others and the world around us through a series of filters or lenses that have more to do with what we think or assume about them than who or what they actually are in any given moment.

- We minimize or ignore the inner thoughts or feelings that alert us to what we really want to do or say in any given moment.

How, then, are we going to sort out the sparks—the information needed to help us come more fully alive—from the ongoing internal clutter?

## Tuning the dial to reduce static

Eastern teachings include the Buddhist concept of "monkey mind," a wonderful metaphor describing the unruly nature of the human mind and its predisposition to swing like a mischievous monkey, without stopping, from one thought to another.[32] To use an electronic metaphor we're all familiar with, it's as if our minds are constantly changing channels, flipping between stations with remarkable speed

---

[32] The Buddhist concept of monkey mind is discussed in many books and Eastern sources. Interested readers could start with Wikipedia by looking up "mind monkey" and going from there. One book offering a good context for working with monkey mind is Yongey Mingyur Rinpoche and Eric Swanson, *The Joy of Living: Unlocking the Secret and Science of Happiness* (New York: Crown Publishing/Harmony Books, 2007).

and varying degrees of attention to what we're hearing, seeing, sensing, and feeling within.

There's nothing wrong with this. It's simply the way our experiential equipment operates, and trying to make the mind behave otherwise is a waste of time and energy that will likely just *add* to the clutter you're already carrying around inside.

Even disciplined, long-term practitioners of meditation experience monkey mind as the backdrop of their daily experience. But by focusing attention and working with the breath, those who regularly practice meditation are gradually able to connect with a place of peaceful awareness that is not distracted by the background noise and antics of monkey mind.

Schools of meditation differ in their approaches, techniques, and goals. If you're curious and want to learn more about meditation, explore the resources we've gathered that are accessible through information given at the back of this book.

Sorting out the sparks from the clutter is like manually adjusting a radio dial: a subtle shift of focus in our attention to locate and tune in to what we're truly feeling, thinking, and experiencing in any given moment. Continuing this radio-dial analogy, it may at first seem challenging to get past the "static" as you try to tune in to the accurate "stations" that identify your authentic internal states. You may need to pause in your daily activities at first, or even come to a full stop, in order to access and make sense of the subtle thoughts and feelings you're not used to paying attention to. As you get more practice in doing so, you'll find yourself developing the ability to do this inner listening and sorting with less effort and disruption to the flow of external events.

The benefits of being able to tune in this way are limitless. By regularly shifting out of autopilot mode and paying fresh and focused attention to the present moment—wherever we are and whatever we're doing—we prime ourselves for noticing sparks, recognizing synchronistic events, and making contact with our deepest needs and wants.

In contrast, when we remain on autopilot, our tendency is to react in familiar ways without even being aware that we have other choices available to us. With a shift in attention and a little practice, it's possible to notice important information we need to chart a new course *and* live more fully in the present moment.

When we truly open ourselves to meeting life on its own terms, embracing the possibility for change in untold new directions, we open the door to adjustments in jobs, careers, living arrangements, lifestyles, relationships, geographical location, and just about everything else. As we begin to listen with increased interest in and respect for our inner voice, we expand our trust in what it reveals to us. Working to clarify and release fears, and paying attention to the sparks that surround us, we slowly loosen our grip on the life we've planned and let go into the life that is waiting for us.[33]

---

### Barbara's story:
### "The horizontal journey"

I recall precisely where I was when I first realized, with an electric and radiating buzz throughout my entire body, that my personal sense of "I" would never be completely free of the distressing and often chaotic world of my inner thoughts. The very idea immediately made me euphoric! At the same moment I realized I would never be free, I was instantly free! It was one of those rare occasions when,

---

[33] The full text of the Joseph Campbell quote referred to is this: "We must be willing to let go of the life we planned so as to have the life that is waiting for us."

without trying or even being aware that I was on the edge of a discovery, I suddenly felt as if my inner self had broken open and was circulating wildly, this time rushing outwards into the dark night air.

It was the winter of 1991, and I was walking along the gravel shoulder of a neighborhood street in a suburb of Winnipeg, Manitoba, during a precious break from my duties as a wife and the mother of two very young children. I was breathing the chilled air, sensing the muscles moving in my arms and legs, and was lost in thought about the most recent chapter I'd read in Joanna Field's classic 1936 book *A Life of One's Own*.[34]

Looking back on that event and other such times, I still cannot adequately express the magnitude of the sensations I felt in my physical body and mind with the arrival of a new and wonderful realization like this. A common term is "mind-blowing," but that's not quite big enough to include the full-body visceral awareness that accompanied it. It's as if the person I had become in that instant was now too large to fit into the dimensions of the physical and mental shell I'd been living in just a moment before. The experience was rarified and fleeting, but it was clear and solid enough to push the reset button on my entire way of thinking.

As I continued to walk that night, allowing my body to settle and my mind to wrap itself around the implications of this new awareness, I retraced my internal steps and considered the impact on my current life. Joanna Field, pseudonym for British author Marion Milner, was describing in *A Life of One's Own* how she had been working her way through a seven-year exploration of her meandering way of thinking, following the ins and outs of her inner material, in pursuit of "discovering one's true likes and dislikes

---

[34] Joanna Field, *A Life of One's Own* (Los Angeles: J. P. Tarcher, 1981).

for finding and setting up a standard of values that is truly one's own and not a borrowed mass-produced ideal."

It was that description on the back cover of the book that had drawn me to it in the first place: Field's awareness that she was not living a truly authentic existence, uncertain as to who she truly was or what she really wanted out of life. The book alluded to a potential rebirth and an actual way to achieve happiness and escape "spiritual virginity." She was expressing my predicament exactly, or at least I thought so at the time.

The initial core of meaning I took home with me that night was a sense of sweet relief in finally knowing, in my body and my deepest sense of self, that the goal was not to continue wrestling with the content of my often erratic thoughts and emotions, hoping to tame them. Nor was it to continue to think or to wish that such problematic data would eventually stop once I was spiritual enough, or sufficiently disciplined enough, or enlightened enough, or whatever else. I was tired and worn down with my own bouts of unhappiness, frustrated with their frequent pestering in my day-to-day existence that interrupted my peace of mind and caused ripples in my relationships. *This*, I finally realized, *would never go away.*

Furthermore, I suddenly understood that the source of these thoughts and emotions was not "me." I also realized that the inner operating system of human beings contains "equipment" that continuously generates thoughts and emotions. This is often not very sophisticated equipment, and we can get hung up on familiar and limited ways of processing the world and what's going on around and within us.

In a whole new way, I clued in to Field's descriptions as the observer of her own inner drama. By seeing what was going on in her through her writing, I was able to make the connection to what was really going on inside of me: that there was a neutral place within the field of consciousness I knew as "me" that was separate from and beyond all the ups and downs of anything I could experience in my body or my mind. This patient observer was aware of everything going on in my personal life, but it wasn't caught up in the drama of it—the drama that's the given dynamic when one is identified with one's personality, including likes, dislikes, biases, preferences, beliefs, and so on. And even though the drama would continue forever, simply as a part of the experience of a human being in a physical body, there is always a place within that is beyond, separate from, and unruffled by the peaks and valleys of daily life.

*Nothing needed to change*, neither in the outside world nor inside me. It was just that I needed to learn how to spend more time with this other location within myself that was aware of a broader context and was less attached to the outcomes of situations. My wrestling match with myself was over.

I was no longer on the road to a "vertical destination," believing that I needed to achieve higher states of consciousness. My path instead became a "horizontal journey" that had everything to do with meeting this neutral, centered, peaceful sense of presence within myself and learning to live from there. I had read about these concepts and understood them in my head, as knowledge, but now I resonated with them in my body and depths, as wisdom, and could earnestly get on with exploring and beginning to live them more fully.

Easier said than done! I'm still working on it, if "working" is the right word, because the cultivation of this inner exploration is a process of letting go of everything else for a while—the ramblings of the mind, the tug of emotions and feelings, the important decisions and struggles in the outside world—and resting in the unfathomable place of quiet that sustains and illuminates our very existence. It requires some discipline to show up and make time for this inner meeting-at-the-edge (of personality, of awareness, of consciousness), but it's not *work* in the way we're used to working.

In the terms we're using in this book, the experience I've just described is probably one of *internal combustion*: it came on with a bang and fueled a new chapter of discovery that is still unfolding in my life. We all have these leaps in awareness, but they don't come often.

An even richer gift is that of the smaller, less explosive but equally valuable sparks that are with us each and every day in the life occurring around and within us. As we seek to recognize these and explore what they might be asking of us—to notice something previously unnoticed, to take an action, to shift our thinking and attitudes, or to accept a new idea that's challenging to us in some way—we open ourselves to the most amazing and profound journey there is: the horizontal journey within.

*I want to unfold.*
*Nowhere do I want to remain folded,*
*because where I am bent and folded, there I am a lie.*
Rainer Maria Rilke, from his poem
"*I Am Too Alone in the World*"

## Sparks in the dark: an invitation to notice and ponder your night dreams

The dreams we have at night are an amazing yet often frustrating part of our human experience. All of us have them, reportedly many dreams each night, but many of us either can't remember them or have trouble making any sense of them when we wake.

Many cultures throughout the ages have placed great emphasis on remembering and sharing the potent stories revealed in dreams. Dreams were often viewed as integral to the health and well-being of both the individual and the community as a whole. These days, it's difficult to pinpoint any one widely accepted mainstream source of explanation or information on dreaming: the topic is perhaps just as controversial and difficult to understand conclusively as it was centuries ago.

It is beyond the scope of this book to address the history of dreaming, the significance of dreams for various cultures, or the diversity of approaches to understanding and working with them to further individual growth and enhance the collective evolution of consciousness. What we would like to offer here is an invitation simply to remain open to the possibility of another invaluable source of sparks: the strange and magnificent images and themes in your dreams.

It may be enough, at first, to begin to incorporate new ways of paying attention to sparks and synchronicity in your *waking* reality, and this is an excellent first step. It takes time to explore and experiment with ideas and practices we haven't previously entertained. And if you're like most, you'll have more success at taking smaller, incremental steps in personal growth than you will if you take on too much at the start. In other words, if it's enough at first to start paying attention to your daily life in new ways—being open to sparks and synchronistic events and learning to tune in more fully to what's going on in the moment—then simply embrace this as your most appropriate place to begin.

When you're ready, however, there's a vibrant universe to be explored in the seemingly real adventures of sleep. We each have, within us, the wisdom and strength to create change in our lives. Our capacity to connect with these rich depths, however, is not as straightforward and easy as we'd wish. Our dreams present us with dramatic scenarios that are symbolic in nature. Their meaning is usually not literal but is instead hinted at through the brilliant use of personally meaningful images and experiences.

Viewed in this way—as a dynamic and interactive resource that can help expand our awareness, make conscious our biases and blinds spots in waking life, and potentially open new doorways to balance and healing—working with your dreams invites a whole new level of exploration and growth.

Often, we shake our heads at the bizarre nature of our dreams or prefer not to think about the stark images or startling events that transpire in the realm of sleep. At times, our dreams can be quite disturbing to us, leading to a desire to silence them and turn off the source. There may be wisdom in this caution, as dreams can sometimes be trying to help us relive and release difficult circumstances from our past or alert us to potentially harmful situations in our present life.

Seeking the assistance and guidance of a professional person experienced in working with dreams (a counselor, therapist, analyst, elder, or other reputable resource person) is a helpful way to face such inner content in an environment of care and support.

## Some beginning tips for working with your dreams

The literature and advice out there on how to remember and interpret dreams is diverse. Some books are explicit and rigid dream dictionaries, sources that offer universal translations of key symbols that commonly occur in dreams, a kind of one-size-fits-all approach. Some offer the more complex and intensive approaches of analytical psychology to guide interpretations and ongoing work with dream images, such as the work of Carl Jung and related Jungian authors and schools of thought.

In general, simple curiosity is a wonderful first step toward inviting this deeper source of wisdom and intelligence to communicate more fully with us. There is an old expression that says: "What you are seeking is also seeking you." If you're going to begin the process of dialogue with the rich, symbolic imagery in your dreams, you're going to need to remember at least a few of the details as they actually happened. This is more challenging than you might think, as dreams tend to slip away at first light, quietly and quickly, back into the depths from which they emerged.

To remember them accurately, we need to catch them by the tail, capturing their essence in as much detail as possible while they're fresh and immediate. Keeping a pen and pad of paper at your bedside is an enormous help, as is a small unobtrusive light such as a book light or miniature flashlight if you're concerned about disturbing a sleeping partner. It's helpful to take enough time to write down *all the details* you can remember, even the seemingly insignificant ones, as they unfolded in the dream.

Once you have the dream's details jotted down, the next step is to find some time during the day to reflect on the images and the story in the dream, re-entering the actions, thoughts, feelings, and sensations in the body as fully as you can. Keeping in mind that the events and characters are symbolic, ask yourself about your associations with these specific details. It's not unlike a game of charades or an episode of a crime-solving TV show, so explore the possible meanings or motives of the characters and their actions and *don't assume you already know what it all means*.

While you might not unlock the layers of meaning inherent in the dream immediately, you may find that later insights will pop up during the course of the day, shedding more light on your dream. Or you may find that further dreams take place, including daydreams, that continue the story or otherwise help you figure out additional clues to unravel the deeper plot.

If you are someone who doesn't remember their dreams, be aware that this is reversible. Begin by inviting the dreams back into your conscious awareness, perhaps by stating an intention when you prepare yourself for sleep. Again, if you are apprehensive about dark or scary images coming to you through the "dream channel," then you might be wise to explore your reservations with a trusted friend or experienced professional.

Don't forget to include daydreams as another wonderful source of insight. When our minds are off wandering around, they are often specific in their destinations! Notice the lyrics to the tune you're humming in your head. What is this song about, and what might it be saying to you right now? Tune in to the details of the scenario unfolding within you that's playing on your inner video screen. Notice where your attention has gone while you were operating in autopilot mode. Your daydreams and night dreams will tell you a lot.[35]

There are countless helpful resources for working with the content of dreams. So that you can find the particular approach that ignites sparks within you, we invite you to explore the links available in the Further Resources section at the back of the book.

All of our inner and outer experiences can tell us more about who we are, what we're doing here, and the location of the most appropriate place to focus our energy and attention. As Carl Jung observed: "Your vision will become clear only when you look into your heart. Who looks outside, dreams. Who looks inside, awakens."

---

[35] A good, user-friendly book to read before beginning work on your own dreams is Robert Bosnak's *A Little Course in Dreams* (Boston: Shambhala Publications, 1986).

Let us share here one of the many stories from the Upside community.

---

### Iwona's story:
### "The Five-Minute Miracle"

Forty years ago
my life reported its last sighting of fairies, angels, miracles.

Since then I have been running from myself:
faster and faster,
jerking to the left and right,
following a track through the ups and downs of school,
work, parenting
and married life.

On I traveled through the flat plains of depression and self-doubt
until I reached the terminal station: "The Designated Accountant."
Running far enough, I forgot what I was, other than
responsibility, schedule, spreadsheet,
and the grocery list.

Throughout my journey there were glimpses in the windows,
joyful moments,
brief stops in pleasant stations:
pregnant with desire, blurry dreams of shapeless forms flying high;
the feeble pursuits of little hobbies on the side,
photography of shadows and spring dew,
stick drawings in a journal,
shy flower paintings.

Nothing serious. These efforts
were klutzy, hidden, handicapped and ultimately aborted.
The great Abortionist: my Fear.

Fear, my omnipotent assistant,
protector of my teeth from rot with daily reminders to
brush,
champion of my kids' futures commanding countless
activities,
caretaker of the family table needing its daily bread to
carry.

Fear: my friend who overstayed too often,
nagging me to move
       faster,
          get more,
              prove myself,
                 provide.
How to excuse a friend who is required for survival
but who stinks after one visit too many?

My Fear brags
(or I for him?)
that he is mighty and invincible.
This very belief the ultimate tomb,
the absolute, illusionary, macro-realm of Never, Always,
Too Old, and Too Late.

His boring speeches so familiar, becoming my gospel:
"You will *never* be a Picasso....
       You will *always* be a boring accountant....
              You are *too old* to give birth to the artist you
                          carry inside....

Just look at you (how can you be so
ridiculous!) ....
At *your* age? It is too late to
even think about it."
This bully has been tolerated long enough!
I have allowed his presence long enough.

This summer,
another erratic turn through the triumph of professional
designation.
And with it pain, my inner healer, pain so intense
living my life as an obligation rather than a miracle,
yesterdays dissolving into tomorrows with nothing in
between.
Pain piercing me sharply enough to demand a change of
direction:
"What is the next station stop? Another title?
Another rung on the corporate ladder?
Another joyless job?
Another badge to prove I am
worthy?"

Worthy of what?
And who is to judge?

My ride came to a standstill, the train running out of
steam.
Waiting for a spark in a directionless haze:
Where to go, what to do.... *Who am I?*
My engine needing a different fuel.
Waiting without knowing it for a wiser conductor
(in the outer form of Steve),
there all along but unobserved, unimagined, uncreated in
my awareness.
Other travelers are necessary on our journey.

They know a different way, are aware of more exciting destinations.
Left on their own, our engines follow old routes, rusted tracks,
conditioned too long with outworn beliefs.
Worn-out minds and stuck synapses needing a spark,
a forceful kick in the gut to recalibrate.

This wise man gave me permission to be both:
an accountant dabbling in art;
     an accountant and a mini-poet;
          a provider and an evanescent dreamer.
Now I am free to cut a red square from the junk mail
and sit it on a swing in my journal, dressing it in a crown
and violet robe.

Being an accountant proves necessary.
It supports blissful ignorance of the utilitarian, marketable
aspects of my joyful little pursuits.
It feeds my babies their daily bread while they limp along,
growing wings ahead of near flight.

A spark was all I needed, a little trick that hovers safely
below the radar
of the bully.
The very idea: for five minutes each day, the freedom to
be an artist.
(My secret dream!)
My Fear friend does not register the lowly five-minute
visitor.
Never and Always are monumental enough to prevail,
to "protect,"
to block and lock me in forever (or so He thinks).

For the last two months—every day—I invite the Five-Minute Miracle.

This new visitor is welcome to overstay!
Shy, non-threatening, inconspicuous
this little, beautiful trick that, once I kick the door open,
always lasts longer than the five intended minutes.

We have so much fun together.

One day this new friend may stay forever!
A little miracle with blue angels,
sprouting on my journal pages and jumping off onto over-sized canvasses.

Maybe the fairies will come back again.

*Iwona is happy to report that, after thirty years of secret longing, she is completely smitten with her new and not-so-secret immersion in brief stints of pure, artistic joy. Her "modified Zen" practice of the Five-Minute Miracle has emboldened her to take a next step: registration in a local, two-month botanical drawing class. "From the spark to the fire: I am on fire and it feels great," she says. "The sparks are flying everywhere!" She credits Steve for helping her to find the way through to this new, integral part of her life.*

# Exercise 5 –
# Noticing sparks and recognizing synchronicity

Synchronicity, as we're defining it here, is the art of being open, alert, and curious within ourselves and towards our surroundings (in synch) so we can observe and attract people and opportunities into our lives that we might otherwise have ignored or missed. This exercise will help you to reflect on the influence of sparks and synchronicity in your life up until now, plus assist you to begin to identify ways to increase your awareness of these elements in your life from here forward.

## Step 1 – Consider your life to date

Take a moment to consider and briefly note below three to five events or situations in your life that were powerful and far-reaching in their impact on you, such as:

- Windfall experiences in which something unexpected and wonderful took place;
- Turning-point experiences when your life suddenly changed focus, direction, and/or meaning from within;
- Devastating circumstances where it seemed like the rug was pulled out from under you and your peace of mind or well-being dissolved for a period of time;
- Eye-opening situations that forever changed your way of thinking about yourself, someone else, and/or the world around you.

1. _____
2. _____
3. _____
4. _____
5. _____

## Step 2 – Note your level of involvement

Take care to note your level of involvement in the occurrence of these events. As you reflect on each of the events or situations you've noted above, ask yourself these questions:

- Did I know or predict this was going to occur before it did?
- What was going on when I first became aware of this event or situation?
- How did I first react or respond to it?
- What impact did this reaction or response have on me and the people around me?
- Was I aware of my reaction or response while I was engaged in it?
- What else was I aware of, around me and within me, while this was going on?
- Over time, what changes did I notice in my thinking and processing of this event or situation?
- Did something that seemed "bad" at the time remain so, or has anything "good" come from it over time? Conversely, did something that seemed "good" at the time remain so, or has anything "bad" come from it since? If so, what?
- Looking back at this time, how much responsibility do I see myself as having in this event or situation taking place? Is this accurate? Are there other influencing elements I can see now that I wasn't able to see at the time? How do I feel about these now as I look at them?
- Were there some other elements taking place, big or small, that, had I noticed them, would have made a difference in the outcome? If so, what prevented me from noticing them at the time?
- Are there some things I can learn from this experience that might help me to be more open to the presence of sparks and synchronicities in my life from here forward? (Take the time to write down these ideas and review them from time to time, especially when something of magnitude takes place in your life.)

- What, from my own experience, do I have to share with others about learning from life's ups and downs? If asked, what advice do I have to offer others?

# Affirmations

- I am beginning to trust more fully what life has to offer and teach me, knowing that I have or will find the resources I need.

- I am increasingly aware of the difference between fear in my mind and fear in my body. When I take the time to gently examine and challenge the fears that arise in my mind, I sort through the real from the imagined and decide for myself how best to meet each situation in my life.

- When I resist the automatic habit of labeling people, situations, and even myself as "good" or "bad," I leave room for seeing and understanding things more clearly and prime myself for finding a new, less-conditioned response to the world around me.

- I am aware of a peaceful and non-judgmental place within that is always with me. By making the time and effort to be with this place of stillness, I can calm my inner world and create the space for balance and healing in my life.

- I am a human *being*, not a human *doing*.

- There is so much more to life that meets the eye. As I learn to honor and respect the unknowable wonders within me—and within others—I open myself to the richness of life and relationships as they unfold in the present moment.

Notes to myself _____

# CHAPTER 5

# The Power of Authentic Giving

### Extending Ourselves to Others in Ways that Make a Difference

You give but little when you give of your possessions.
It is when you give of yourself that you truly give.

KAHLIL GIBRAN

I often joke that if you really want to be selfish, you should be generous! You should take good care of others, be concerned for their welfare, help them, serve them, make more friends, make more smiles. The result...? When you yourself need help, you'll find plenty of helpers.

HIS HOLINESS THE FOURTEENTH DALAI LAMA

Each relationship you have with another person
reflects the relationship you have with yourself.

ALICE DEVILLE

The place to improve the world is first in one's own heart and head and hands, and then work outward from there.

ROBERT M. PIRSIG

W e've talked a lot in previous chapters about methods and the importance of nurturing your own mind and body to find the Upsides each day and remain upbeat, optimistic, and sufficiently resilient to meet whatever circumstances life brings. But this is only part of the equation to a fuller and happier life. Engaging in activities that reach out to others, especially when you are able to connect with those who benefit from your efforts, is powerful for both the giver and the receiver.

---

### Sharon's story:
### "Reminding others that they matter"

I "woke up" recently when I received an email from a friend that simply said: "I'm thinking of you, and I miss you. Thank you for being YOU." That simple, loving note, with the sentiment of Mister Rogers' famous phrase, "I like you just the way you are," made my day on one of those days when I really needed to hear it.

I realized how often I thought about people who were important and special in my life and how I didn't make a practice of telling them. On that day, I decided to begin sending emails or cards to those people to tell them I was thinking of them and to convey just how they were special to me.

It's really quite amazing to see the way these individuals responded to the notes and how my messages arrived on a day and at a time when they most needed to know they were thought of and cared for. I have since shared this idea with many others and they, in turn, have had the same experience. We don't ever get over needing to know we are loved and that we matter in this world.

---

## Simple Giving with Profound Results

Sharon's story about reminding others they matter illustrates the power that seemingly small gifts can have when they come from the heart, as an extension of who we each uniquely are. "We don't ever get over needing to know we are loved," Sharon says, "and that we matter in this world." But how do we figure out what giving from the heart actually means?

The topic of giving—of contributing to others' lives in meaningful ways—is a complex one. When we talk about giving, making contributions and/or donations, being of service, giving back, doing things for others, lending a hand, involving ourselves in charitable work, supporting a cause, and so on, we're touching on a multifaceted range of intentions and actions. There are as many ways to give as there are individuals on this planet.

In addition to being complex, the topic of giving is also a fairly loaded one in that it touches deeply into the core beliefs, values, and expectations we hold for others and ourselves.

Most of us believe that it's a good thing to do our part in making our communities and the world a better place to live in. But how much time, energy or money should we each spend? On whom or what? How often? In what ways? How do we choose? Do we wait until we're asked to give? How do we know our giving is helping? How do we know when our gifts are enough? If you start up a conversation in which you politely ask some pointed questions about the form this giving should take, you'll soon notice the signs and signals that you're entering into potentially controversial territory.

One of the trickiest aspects to giving is the motive behind the gift, as illustrated in this excerpt from Kahlil Gibran's *The Prophet*,[36] first published in 1923:

---

[36] Kahlil Gibran, *The Prophet* (New York: Alfred A. Knopf, 1985).

*There are those who give little*
*of the much which they have –*
*and they give it for recognition*
*and their hidden desire*
*makes their gifts unwholesome.*
*And there are those who have little and give it all.*
*These are the believers in life and the bounty of life,*
*and their coffer is never empty.*
*There are those who give with joy,*
*and their joy is their reward.*
*And there are those who give with pain,*
*and that pain is their baptism.*
*And there are those who give and know not*
*pain in giving, nor do they seek joy,*
*nor give with mindfulness of virtue:*
*They give as in yonder valley the myrtle*
*breathes its fragrance into space.*
*Through the hands of such as these God*
*speaks, and from behind their eyes*
*He smiles upon the earth.*

## Authentic giving

Are some ways of giving better than others? Who gets to decide? Even to attempt to figure out what authentic giving means and what it would look like, someone would have to come up with a definition. The word points to adjectives like sincere, genuine, without pretense, not feigned or affected, true, and honestly felt or experienced. You might want to come up with your own definition, one that authentically fits for you.

Most of us, as adults, dislike being told what to do. If we're in a learning environment and are keen to grasp what's being taught, we're likely to be open to doing things in the new way we're being shown. Rather than having someone else tell you what authentic giving to others should look like and how it ought to be done, why not begin today to trust yourself to figure it out? How can you give in ways that are sincere, authentic, genuine, and honestly felt by you?

The feedback we're receiving from people engaged in the Finding the Upside process, whether in workshops or through the electronic forums on the Upside website, is that they are surprised, delighted, and profoundly moved to discover new ways of giving back and making a difference in the lives of others. As they were moved inwardly to reach out in some tangible way to another, be it a person, an organization, a cause, a community, or nature, they found themselves opening up to new sources of quiet wonder and boisterous joy through their giving. In some mysterious way, it isn't the size or the form of the gift that matters so much as it is the place from which the gift originates. And it's the degree to which we allow ourselves to follow the new path that is created through the giving and the receiving.

In the words of Ralph Waldo Emerson, "It is one of the most beautiful compensations of this life that no man can sincerely try to help another without helping himself."

Let us share a few more of the stories from the Upside community—this time from Rosa, Agnes, and Steve.

---

### Rosa's story:
### "The gift of one Upside leading to another"

I've recently experienced the satisfaction of giving back and making a difference, and it has made a powerful transformation in my life. In the past year, I've gone from feeling deep despair and shame about my adult son's substance abuse problem to a sense of empowerment and hope for his recovery. I cannot take full credit for the changes, since I know that a higher power led me to where I am today. What is most amazing to me is how liberated I feel today, for this has given me renewed energy to continue to help him and myself.

Looking back, I was devastated for several years by my son's problem and my inability to help him. I felt a great loss, since I had such high hopes and expectations for my only son. I felt helpless and ashamed that somehow I had failed as a parent.

I was also going through my own inner turmoil at the time as I reflected on the shattered path of my marriage (my husband of twenty years and I divorced when my son was twelve) and how, since then, I had devoted all my energies to raising my son. The result of these combined issues was an identity crisis: I didn't know who I was besides a failed mother and a failed spouse, without a real passion or interest for much else besides my son's recovery. Unbeknownst to me, my recovery began to take shape alongside his.

It started in early 2008 when I briefly traveled from New Jersey to Florida to visit my son. He had completed an intensive therapy/recovery program and was transitioning to living at All the Way House, King's Haven, in what would typically be called a halfway house. I didn't know quite what to expect but, as it turned out, the place was a love-filled home where the residents were encouraged to go *all the way* with their recovery, not just half of the way, which is the standard at many similar centers.

My initial intention was to limit my visits to a day or two—just to say hello and to keep in touch—but I became more and more involved in his new life in recovery, gradually developing relationships with the other guys in his program who were all going through this together. My trips became more frequent and progressively longer, and I witnessed first-hand the wonderful transformation that was happening in my son's life as well as in the lives of the other men in his program.

I was welcomed into their world and found I'd become a source of encouragement for them. I'd help out in small ways: cook meals, play tennis, attend church services, offer career advice, all the while giving them time and attention because I valued them. I didn't know it at the time, but they were also giving me a renewed sense of purpose, the higher purpose that I'd long been searching for.

The highlight of my involvement occurred this past summer when it was apparent that the center was operating at full capacity and needed additional space. I was motivated to help them and initially offered to put down the deposit that would allow them to rent a newer, larger home. Within a period of two months, however, I went from the offer to lend them the start-up funds to actually making a personal investment and buying them a house!

The Upside of the current economic downturn was that I was able to find a foreclosed home in mint condition for about 25 percent of its selling price three years earlier. This new and larger location gives hope to an additional eight men in active recovery. My son and his roommates were able to furnish the new home tastefully with donated items from church members, and all have taken much pride in their new surroundings.

Another dimension of my transformation is that I have evolved into a new life in Florida and am thinking of making it a more permanent home. I've met many wonderful people who are compatible with various facets of my life and with whom I feel I can continue to grow. I've even seen my small investment give hope to the community of neighbors and business people because of my demonstration of confidence in the future of recovery and real estate during such a difficult economic time.

As I reflect on my Upside transformation, moving from a place of feeling the weight of adversity to a renewed sense of hopefulness over the past year, I have gained some valuable insights about my personal journey that might be helpful to others going through comparable challenging situations with their health, relationships, work, finances, or other aspects of their lives. Here's what I'd like to share from my own journey:

- **Give yourself time to experience your negative feelings.** Had I not spent several years in anguish over my son's situation, I doubt I would have appreciated my recovery as fully.

- **Surround yourself with a non-judgmental circle of confidants who do not blame you for your problems.** By going to Florida, I met new people who saw me differently than my traditional friends did and felt more liberated to express myself authentically in my new situation.

- **Trust your feelings when you suddenly begin to feel positive and then take specific action in that direction.** At first, it felt awkward to start to feel better about my situation. I was beginning to take control of my life, not the other way around as I'd been living for so long.

- **Be open-minded and embrace new people, situations, and life models.** I realized that part of the reason I felt as badly as I did was that I was comparing myself and my son to many people around me, including those who had their nuclear families intact and those with well-adjusted children who were succeeding academically. I was judging myself against a standard that was impossible for me to achieve, given my circumstances.

■ **Give yourself the opportunity to engage in your passions, the things you like to do, even if it seems weird to the people who think they know you.** As I began to embrace the All the Way community, I regained a sense of purpose I hadn't experienced for a while. I didn't feel I could openly discuss what I was doing with my traditional friends back home, who were cautioning me I was doing something very risky in getting involved with "those types of people." Even my son's therapist warned me that what I was doing by getting so involved was jeopardizing my son's recovery. In retrospect, I feel that I was helping his recovery by setting an example for him of how our generosity can inspire and motivate others.

---

### Agnes's story:
### "Upsiding in action:
### finding and sharing light in the darkness"

I now consider myself an Upsider, embracing a new way to experience life and getting out the Upside message to those I know. Am I there on the Upside all the time, always up and carefree? Heck no, but that's not what I consider the Upside life to be about. I've learned that it's most important to be on the journey: taking on difficult and challenging situations and finding ways to invite and create the positive. In other words, to engage in the act of reaching up.

I didn't just happen upon this Upside perspective as a philosophical pursuit. I encountered the idea in the spring of 2009 while visiting a friend in another state the day after my first breast biopsy. The procedure had ended up being more painful than anticipated, but I decided to go ahead and make the trip anyway, as planned. That's when I attended a free lecture given by Steve Goldberg at the local library in Delray Beach, Florida.

Free is good these days because my job recently disappeared—an experience familiar to so many others in 2009 as a result of the recession—and I was feeling the effects on both my finances and my self-esteem. And that wasn't even the start of it all for me regarding my encounters with the darker side of life over this past year. I'd been working hard to get my emotional house of cards back into some semblance of order after going through the first anniversary of the tragic death of my beautiful godchild and only niece, a death that deeply impacted my entire family. That's when the unexpected downsizing notice descended upon my workplace.

It seems you can have just one thing happen that can shake your world, or you can have a series that topple it with the force of a tsunami. My faith is strong, but those two things hit hard. And then I found out a few months later that I had breast cancer. And around the same time as the surgery, I also had to deal with the end of the significant relationship with my partner of two years.

It was almost too much to bear. As I see it now, it was a dark-night-of-the-soul experience, one that permits me to say that I now have a much better understanding of others who have lived through such times in their lives. If you have been there, you know. If you have truly tasted it on any level, you know.

Before all this turbulence, I used to put such a positive spin on things: the theme of the children's story about the little engine that could; the mindset of looking at the glass as half full rather than half empty; being there for others;

trying my best to give my all, even when the going was difficult.

While those are not bad things to aspire to, I now find I'm coming from a very different place in my interactions with others. All the challenges and personal pain I've lived with recently has tempered me, making me better at being there with people who are still in those tough places or are haunted by earlier losses. It's not the same positive-spin process I used to engage in. I don't expect others just to grin and bear it or to think happy thoughts and immediately get on the Upside of things, because I am uncomfortable with where they might be right now and because I so want for them to be in a better place.

Here's what I've found:

- When we share our own stories, we are more authentic; our personal truths resonate with and inspire others.

- We have a choice each day, sometimes moment to moment, to see where we are, to accept the reality of our situation, take an action, and realize that getting to the Upside of life is a process.

- Sometimes finding the Upside can be as simple as a shift in thinking, the accepting of another's help, or the seeking out of new information that can be put into use.

- For me, the process included reaching out beyond myself by doing something for others, sharing helpful ideas and encouragement, and being grateful for what I have (not just the material possessions) instead of focusing on what was lost.

Maybe you're thinking this is the last thing you have the time, means, talent, energy, money, health, courage, or heart to do. Yet it is often the seemingly small steps and inward shifts that can result in a big ripple in your life, and in others' lives too, in ways you've never dreamed of. I'm talking about my own personal experience here, because shortly after meeting Steve at the library presentation and learning about the Upside perspective, I came across an opportunity through one of my professional networks to volunteer my human resource skills and experience. The invitation was to participate in a series of career workshops and coaching sessions in Fort Dix, N.J., to help prepare soldiers returning from active service for jobs in the current turbulent marketplace.

This was to be a landmark workforce-readiness event, the first of its kind in the area to support service members who had recently returned from duty. The call for volunteers invited career coaches, recruiters, and professionals in the learning and development and human resource fields to offer their time and encouragement and share their specialized knowledge with as many as 750 service men and women.

Even though I was in the midst of my own personal upheaval, I knew I could do this. I felt that if my professional community was willing to be so supportive of the needs of these military personnel, I wanted to contribute. It was personally rewarding for me and the other volunteers to interact with these individuals who had put so much of themselves on the line during their tours of duty. I realized that it was they who had been giving back to us all year round, not to mention the additional sacrifices of their families and friends as they hoped and waited for the safe return of their loved ones. I truly appreciated their contributions and, at the same time, felt their gratitude for our assistance during their transition to a next job or career.

Living and working with the Upside is not a finite destination but a continuous work-in-progress, with many life-shifting experiences along the way. In my experience so far, I've found that when we get beyond ourselves, we end up getting so much in return. I'm also finding some really enjoyable new company as I move along on this journey. In my efforts to move through the challenges to a space of more joy, peace, and contentment in my life, I'm finding myself drawn to becoming part of the chain of those seeking to be there for others. By helping to bring light into the lives of others, I'm lighting up my own world and finding so much to be passionate about. And this is just the beginning!

---

### Steve's story:
### "Giving is the shortest distance to feeling fully alive"

Like many in my generation, I lived my formative years in the 1960s and early '70s as a social activist, believing I was making a difference in the world. My feeling today is that it is even more critical now for us to reawaken a similar vision and commitment. Perhaps more so than at any time in recent history, there is a huge call to action required of each of us. My sense is that a first step is in the direction of living more lightly on our planet, including making a personal choice to live effectively within our individual means.

In my experience, giving back renews energy rather than depleting it and provides a sense of purpose, meaning, and belonging. We can contribute money, our time, and/or our expertise. Each of us can afford to give within our ability. It is up to us, as individuals, to be the best judge of where, when, to whom, and to what extent we have room to give. The truth, however, is that most of us are undercontributing.

■ **Give, but don't give yourself away.** These days, I try to balance my own giving with checks and balances to ensure that I'm not giving myself away, something I have done in the past. I currently spend my volunteer time helping support affordable housing initiatives in my local community. Previously, I spent a number of years volunteering in Africa working in AIDS prevention. I'm a firm believer in this: giving is the shortest distance to feeling fully alive. In finding something to do that reaches beyond ourselves, we discover the key to living a full and fulfilling life.

My work offers me both immediate and longer-term feedback, and in that, I'm very fortunate. It's been especially heartening to have a number of clients write to me recently about their feelings of fulfillment and gratitude for the time we've spent together clarifying and prioritizing what really matters in their lives. Especially in these times, I find this very rewarding and reinforcing feedback.

■ **Even the small gifts count.** I was recently reminded of the wonderful ripple effects that are possible even with small gifts of our time and resources. During a regular visit to my local blood donation unit last spring, I was approached to make an additional donation of red blood cells. This is a bit longer procedure, but it helps in the treatment of children with cancer. The donor clinic happened to be offering a free movie ticket to donors.

Emerging from my donor experience, I felt like a triple winner: I did something I felt good about; I gave back to a needed cause; and I was able to pass on my movie ticket to someone who had just lost their job and needed a boost. Donating blood is an example of something simple that any of us can do, and the need is great in communities everywhere in the world. If you are unsure of where to begin with respect to giving back in your own community, why not start with this no-cost, invaluable gift of your own resources. You'll literally be giving from your heart.

---

## Questions for reflection

- Am I comfortable with the ways and the extent to which I give back to others and the world around me?

- If not, what comes to mind as I tune in to my thoughts and feelings about this topic?

- Are there some new ideas that have come to me about ways to contribute to others' lives as a result of reading this chapter?

- If so, what are these and what, exactly, sparked within me when I first read or heard them? How can I build on these sparks?

## Affirmations

- There are endless ways to contribute to the people and organizations that are helping to create the change I hope to see in the world. When I take the time to focus inward and determine how I feel best about giving in any situation, I give of myself—with clarity and genuineness—regardless of how the gift is received.

- Small gifts from the heart can be just as rich and meaningful as big gifts from the wallet.

- When I trust in life as it unfolds moment by moment, I know that opportunities will arise wherein I will be just the right person, at the right time, to offer the kind of help that will make a beneficial difference. May I be open to these opportunities and take notice when they occur, knowing I always have a choice in how and when I respond.

■ I myself can put into action the advice of Robert M. Pirsig: "The place to improve the world is first in my own heart and head and hands, and then work outward from there."

Notes to myself _____

_____
_____
_____
_____
_____
_____
_____
_____
_____
_____
_____
_____
_____
_____
_____
_____
_____
_____
_____
_____
_____
_____
_____
_____
_____
_____

# CHAPTER SIX

# Where the Rubber Meets the Road

## Meeting Life with an Upside Attitude, No Matter What

The foolish man seeks happiness in the distance,
the wise man grows it under his feet.

JAMES OPPENHEIM

The breeze at dawn has secrets to tell you. Don't go back to sleep.
You must ask for what you really want. Don't go back to sleep.
People are going back and forth across the doorsill
where the two worlds touch.
The door is round and open. Don't go back to sleep.

JALALUDDIN RUMI

Many men go fishing all of their lives without
Knowing that it is not fish they are after.

HENRY DAVID THOREAU

We began this book from a place of imagination, with a poetic invitation to envision yourself living life in a full and balanced way: valuing your unique path, trusting your insides, taking care of yourself and your relationships, being open to life's changing circumstances, celebrating the wonder and mystery of being alive, and learning and growing as you navigate the ups and downs along the way. The concluding line of the poem leading into the book's introduction offers the suggestion that being you can include all of the components above—as well as the richness of meeting life in the present moment *and* living it to the fullest as you find the Upsides in both its gifts and its challenges.

What we are hoping as we bring this book to a close is that in your journey through the pages—in your personal encounter with the ideas, exercises, reflections, and stories we've presented—you've come to see that experiencing life in this way is indeed possible. The inherent attributes and intentions described in those opening lines are not the improbable and wistful content of dreamy greeting cards. They represent a practical, grounded, and embodied way of living that honors the spiritual and the secular, the inner and the outer, the past and future, the individual and the collective.

## The middle road: trusting life while doing our part

A visit to the self-help department of any bookseller will reveal an abundant array of titles similar to this book: offering advice and testimonials on diverse ways to grow and develop your life in new directions.

Many books in the self-help genre suggest that you first need to construct a clear idea of how things could be or should be in your life (discovering and defining your dream life or your true purpose), then follow through by doing whatever you must do to change things to this other (better) way. This is a tall order. It places the onus on you to figure out an ideal life and then somehow make it happen. The subtle message inherent in such an approach is this: no matter what life presents, you have to continue to strive forward in the direction of your intended destination—and not settle for less. Agree? But in your life experience to date, is this an accurate or realistic reflection of how things have worked for you or others close to you?

Another tangent of the self-help spectrum suggests that everything that happens in our day-to-day life is a reflection of our personal thoughts and intentions. Translation? That we create our own reality. If your life is fraught with difficulties, they are therefore of your own making, so if you change your thinking, your reality will change along with it. This perspective makes a certain amount of sense, yet it's harder to fathom in certain circumstances. When one considers a young child with a fatal illness or birth defect, for instance, did the child create this situation with his or her young thinking?

Other schools of thought suggest that our current life circumstances have little to do with what we've been thinking and everything to do with what we did or didn't do in a previous lifetime. Variations along this continuum state that our current life is the result of our personal fate, or of destiny, or of the decisions of a deity.

The point is that we can get so caught up in philosophy and speculation and the complications of choosing a "right" path (or debating over what's right and what's wrong) that we never get far enough out of our own heads to discover what really fits us in a deep and authentic way.

What we hope we have been able to offer you in *Finding the Upside* are multitudes of sparks to trigger ignition, restarting the process of opening yourself to meeting your life and everything in it—today and in whatever way—with a new kind of acceptance and curiosity. We don't mean a *particular* type of acceptance and curiosity, which implies a specific path or technique that, if used as prescribed, will end up at a predictable destination. We mean your own creative approach to starting to trust that life, in its own unique way of interacting with you, will help you find the next step in your journey.

We are offering you a range of ideas and other catalysts, in other words, to help you get started on the middle road of trusting that life is unfolding as it should—while at the same time remembering that it is up to us as individuals to respond to life's circumstances with awareness and integrity, consciously aligning with our deeper nature as we explore the options before us and choose our thoughts, words, and actions. As we do so, we fulfill our part in living life to the fullest, as best we're able to, whether times are easy or hard.

Here's the thing: you don't need to have it all figured out before you begin, nor do you need to abandon or discard the current circumstances or belief systems already present in your life. Just start where you are now. Review the ideas and suggestions in the book and try them for yourself. If you like what you experience, keep on trying new experiments, checking in and making adjustments as you go.

## Finding the Upside

Let's revisit the last line of the introductory poem once more:

*Being you—meeting life in the present moment*
*and finding the upside in both its gifts and its challenges—*
*allowing life to unfold and living it to the fullest.*

The tangible invitation in these lines, and in the way of meeting life that's suggested in this book, is to arrive at a grounded place within ourselves where we're able not only to find the capacity to accept the circumstances that life is presenting us with but where we can also be open to the potentially positive elements in any situation...

- Even when we can't see or feel anything positive in the present moment as it is, now;
- Even when we can't sense where our current circumstances are leading and whether we'll be better off or worse;
- Even when we're scared or anxious about what might come next;
- Even when it feels foreign and uncomfortable to let go of our usual desire to control the situation and control the others involved;
- Even when we're not sure we can "trust our biology" and our inner intelligence sufficiently to interpret the sparks and synchronicities occurring around and within us that will lead us out of the current challenges to some new situation down the road.

By learning to lean into this new way of being, we set the stage for cultivating resilience, balance, and inspiration in daily life.

## Where the rubber meets the road

This then, as they say, is where the rubber meets the road. This is the time and place where we test things out for ourselves, put theory into action, and see if ideas can become reality. As you near the end of this book and are preparing to finish it and set it aside, now is the appropriate time to determine what, if anything, you'll take away with you from its pages. It's a time not unlike the edge of the dream world when we wake from it (whether it's a dream at night or a book while we're reading it), when the things we experienced while in that trancelike world were vibrant and meaningful but now are fading, slipping away as daily life rushes in to grab our attention.

The natural human tendency is follow the monkey mind on its merry way to the next attraction or distraction. In our haste to move on, many sparks are often left unnoticed on the side of the path, dimming into non-existence as we catch a glimpse of the next compelling object in our line of inner or outer sight.

Care and cultivation are needed if you are going to invite some of the ideas in the book to grow within you in a way that allows you to more fully embody them in your life. Let us offer a few pointers that may help you explore the ideas we've offered, especially those that generated sparks for you and ignited your imagination.

## Things to keep in mind as you travel

- **Stress is an inevitable part of life.** Both the ups and the downs that come our way are equally valid and valuable in experiencing and learning from life. There is no fully effective way to stop or eliminate the pressures of the world. Not only is this impossible, but even trying to is a waste of time and effort. While we cannot control what life brings to our door, nor even the full extent of the consequences of our actions, we are completely free to choose our responses to situations. With exploration and experience, we can learn how to avoid making things worse for ourselves. Stress is not the enemy; it is a part of life. There are countless ways to deal more effectively with stress so that it doesn't narrow our options and impact our health and well-being. No one else can do this part for us.

■ **Thinking is an inevitable part of being human.** Just as there will always be stressors on us from the outside world, there will always be thoughts running through our minds within us. Similarly, we can no more stop life from unfolding "out there" than we can stop our minds from thinking. (Try for a moment to think about *nothing*.... How did you do?) Thinking is not really a problem in itself, but whether or not we're aware of the contents of our thoughts, they do influence our emotions and actions. Pessimistic, fearful, or otherwise limiting thinking can undermine our best efforts at finding and growing the Upsides in life. Runaway thoughts can lead to the creation of convincing stories that will shape our emotions and close us off from new ideas and actions that might be beneficial for us. And watch out for the mental construction of False Evidence Appearing Real. Remember F.E.A.R.? Reduce your use of mental and emotional autopilot, and sense into as many present moments as you can so you notice, fully, your experience in the here and now.

■ **The best things in life are not things.** If you don't believe this yet, experiment! Survivors of tragedies and disasters commonly remark on how terrifying and heartbreaking it is to experience the loss or near-loss of loved ones or other significant relationships. Research is now illustrating how important to our well-being the connections are that we have with others. How might simplifying your life and finding additional ways to enjoy time and connection with others enrich your existence? Ask yourself this the next time you preoccupy your time and energy with the unquestioning pursuit of—*more*.

■ **Change sometimes requires time and effort.** When you were learning to walk, you fell down many times a day. Once you learned to walk, it became second nature, and you likely didn't think much about falling from that point on. If you accomplished all this while you were still a toddler, imagine what you can do now as a fully functioning adult. When you start a new program of exercise, you start with moderation and gradually build on your efforts, knowing it takes time and effort to obtain the results you seek. This kind of incremental progress is also available to you while establishing new practices in your daily mental, emotional, and spiritual life. Remember the minutes-a-day suggestion earlier in this book? The number of minutes isn't critical—but remembering to keep revisiting the ideas and practices that spark your interest *is* important. Experiment with finding a balance between the free-flowing movement of your day as it unfolds and the discipline of making time for the practices that add peace, joy, contentment, relaxation, play, awareness, and inspiration to your life.

■ **Resistance is normal.** Hand-in-hand with the human experience is a common phenomenon called psychological resistance. This term refers to the various ways we knowingly and unknowingly trip ourselves up or undermine our progress when it comes to exploring new aspects of our character and personality, changing the way we think about or do things, setting new personal or professional goals, and so on. We each have our fixed and habitual ways of seeing and being in the world, and resistance is an automatic tendency to stay with these familiar ways and avoid the potential strain or pain of experiencing or doing things differently. Keep an eye out for your own personal forms of resistance when you're attempting to set new positive initiatives going in your life. This could show up as sudden boredom, disinterest, forgetting or being late for important commitments, or engaging in other distractions that are not responding to life's movement but are instead thwarting your intentions and efforts to grow and change. When this occurs, check to see if resistance might be present. If so, don't beat yourself up, because it's a common obstacle along the path. Notice what you've been up to, decide whether it's been helpful, and reset your intentions. Pat yourself on the back for noticing how this works in you, and carry this learning forward into your experience the next time resistance shows up.

- **What doesn't kill us, makes us stronger.** This old saying could be interpreted in its most unpleasant extreme, but none of us would prefer such a painful degree of learning from our experience. A central theme in this book is the idea that challenging times can trigger us to become more resourceful and resilient individuals. Furthermore, as we develop the skills to become more resilient, we actually help protect ourselves from the devastating negative effects of future challenges. In essence, as we become more aware of how stressors affect us and more resourceful in how we respond to them, we enhance our ability to bounce back from negative life experiences. It's important to remember that we can't do this alone: a key element involved is having supportive and caring relationships that offer encouragement when we're down and reassurance when we're feeling shaky. These connections help us to grow our resilience, especially belief in our ability to get through the present circumstances as well as challenging times down the road.

- **Life is a journey, not a destination.** When we let go of ideas of reaching up to attain some imagined standard or to get to some new (higher) level of growth or spiritual attainment, we relax our grip on the old measures related to performance and hierarchy. When we contemplate the concept of having *enough* in life, without being fixated on comparisons to more or less, we can create space for the more *horizontal* journey of being okay as we are, here and now, to meet life as it is, here and now. We simply remain present, curious, and open to both "success" and "failure" in our path from here on. We decide to be gentle with ourselves, patient with our progress, and increasingly comfortable with the idea that this is a whole life's work. Life is occurring—around us, within us and through us—one moment at a time. There's no point hanging onto the past or rushing toward an imagined future. This is an ongoing journey that we each uniquely navigate to the best of our ability.

- **We don't have to do it alone.** It could be that at this point, you don't know anyone else who thinks like you do or similarly to the ideas in this book, but that doesn't mean like-minded people don't exist. If it's true that in this universe, what we focus on expands (test this out for yourself!), then chances are that you'll soon meet other Upside thinkers. The buddy system of connecting with others works on several levels, including perspective (another person can offer different insights or points of view); new ideas (two heads can be better than one when it comes to brainstorming); support (which includes encouragement when the going gets tough and sharing in the celebration when the hurdle is overcome); and accountability (the ability to persevere improves when we share our intentions with another and check in regularly with each other regarding progress). Supportive and caring connections with others are integral to our overall health and well-being. If your current supply of positive and encouraging people in your life is low, it's time to plant new seeds. Check out the Further Resources section in this book to link to additional meet-up sites and activities; participate in the *Starting Your Week on the Upside* weblog; or sign up for a workshop or class in your local area that explores similar concepts. Many of the resources in your community and online are low-cost or no-cost.

- **Make time for play.** According to Stuart Brown, author of *Play: How It Shapes the Brain, Opens the Imagination, and Invigorates the Soul*,[37] play-deprived adults are often rigid, humorless, inflexible, and closed to trying out new options. A healthy dose of playfulness enhances our capacity to innovate, adapt, and master changing circumstances. Play is not an escape; it can actually help us to integrate and reconcile difficult or contradictory situations. It can even show us a way out of our problems. (Think of a time when you came back from vacation full

---

[37] Stuart Brown, M.D., Play: How It Shapes the Brain, Opens the Imagination, and Invigorates the Soul (New York: Penguin Group, 2009).

of new ideas and inspiration to tackle your home life or work life.) If it's true that the smarter the animal, the more they play, as Stuart Brown says, then how are you measuring up as an intelligent human being? Make time for play in your daily life. It will help you to reshape any rigid views and get you in touch with the joyful core of your being.

## Blessings for your journey

We would like to close by offering you a few more thoughts to light your path and accompany you along the way. So many wonderful and inspirational words and verses have been written, stretching back to times of antiquity, and the following are only a few. You can gather up more that resonate with you. We invite you, as you travel, to search out the passages that nurture your soul. Keep these treasures within reach to renew yourself with their themes and rhythms, especially during times of struggle. Blessings on your journey…

## On celebrating your unique path

*Begin by accepting where you are.*
*We all have special gifts of character.*
*Some of us are blessed with compassion; others, laughter;*
*others, a power of self-discipline.*
*Some of us are filled with the beauty of people, others with*
*the beauty of nature.*
*Some of us have a keen sense of the injustices in life;*
*others are drawn to celebrate the goodness around us.*
*These are all starting points, because they are all places of belief.*
*You must find the gift that you have—the source of your*
*belief—and discover a way to cultivate that gift…*

*Do not refuse to seek God because you cannot find the one truth.*
*We live in a pluralistic world, and only the most hard-headed people re-*
*fuse to accept the fact that truth—whether spiritual, cultural, political,*
*or otherwise—is given to different people in different ways.*
*Find the path that glows like a sunlit day, rich in remembered scents and*
*promises. Then follow. Only a fool refuses to walk in the sunlight because*
*he cannot see the shape of the sun.*

Kent Nerburn,[38]
writing in the twentieth century

## On choosing your companions

*Be with those who help your being.*
*Don't sit with indifferent people, whose breath*
*    comes cold out of their mouths.*
*Not these visible forms, your work is deeper.*
*A chunk of dirt thrown in the air breaks to pieces.*
*If you don't try to fly, and so break yourself apart,*
*    you will be broken open by death,*
*        when it's too late for all you could become.*
*Leaves get yellow. The tree puts out fresh roots*
*    and makes them green.*
*Why are you so content with a love that turns you yellow?*

Jalaluddin Rumi,[39]
writing in the thirteenth century

---

[38] Kent Nerburn, Simple Truths: Clear & Gentle Guidance on the Big Issues in Life (Novato, CA: New World Library, 1996).

[39] Maulana Jalal Al-Din Rumi, These Branching Moments: Forty Odes by Rumi, translated by John Moyne and Coleman Barks. (Providence, RI: Copper Beech Press, 1987).

## On setting your bearings

*The warrior's approach is to say "yes" to life: "yea" to it all.*
*Participate joyfully in the sorrows of the world.*
*We cannot cure the world of its sorrows,*
     *but we can choose to live in joy.*
*When we talk about settling the world's problems, we're barking up*
     *the wrong tree.*
*The world is perfect. It's a mess. It has always been a mess.*
*We are not going to change it.*
*Our job is to straighten out our own lives.*

Joseph Campbell,
writing in the twentieth century

## On finding your pace

*A white explorer in Africa, anxious to press ahead with his journey, paid his porters for a series of forced marches. But they, almost within reach of their destination, set down their bundles and refused to budge. No amount of extra payment would convince them otherwise. They said they had to wait for their souls to catch up.*

Bruce Chatwin,[40]
writing in the twentieth century

## On discovering your own wisdom

*There is nothing but water in the holy pools.*
*I know, I have been swimming in them.*
*All the gods sculpted of wood or ivory can't say a word.*
*I know, I have been crying out to them.*

---

[40] Bruce Chatwin, The Songlines (New York: Penguin Books, 1987).

*The Sacred Books of the East are nothing but words.*
*I looked through their covers one day sideways.*
*What Kabir talks of is only what he has lived through.*
*If you have not lived through something, it is not true.*

Kabir,[41]
writing in the fifteenth century

## Notes to myself _____

_____

_____

_____

_____

_____

_____

_____

_____

_____

_____

_____

_____

_____

_____

_____

_____

_____

[41] Kabir was writing primarily in the fifteenth century, and his poems are known in many languages. Rabindranath Tagore, for example, assisted by Evelyn Underhill, translated many from the Sanskrit into English. The versions by Robert Bly presented here are published as The Kabir Book: Forty-four of the Ecstatic Poems of Kabir (Boston: The Seventies Press, 1977).

# The Upside Life Assessment

The Upside Life Assessment (ULA) is a brief personal assessment tool designed to help provide a broad overview of the factors connected with true personal wealth across five distinct dimensions.

By expanding the definition of wealth beyond the more traditional markers we're all familiar with, our goal is to stimulate a deeper investigation of the personal sense of worth and wealth that each of us holds so we can begin to see the true impact these concepts have on our overall sense of well-being.

Basically, the ULA will assist you with determining your perceived level of satisfaction and success in five distinct Upside Wealth Accounts:

- Financial Security and Outlook Account
- Health and Well-Being Account
- Personal Clutter Account
- Relationship with Self and Other Account
- Being Part of the World Account

## Completing the Upside Life Assessment

Once you have completed the assessment, you will have identified some of the areas in your life and among your priorities that may be out of balance and could benefit from further fine-tuning. To assist you with this, we have created a rich library of online and other resources that we trust will spark your interest and enrich your journey. (See Further Resources for Finding the Upside.)

You will find the Upside Life Assessment at www.upsidematters.org/premium. Take a few moments today to access the ULA and get started on your personal journey to real wealth and well-being in all facets of your life.

# Further Resources for Finding the Upside

If some of the ideas in this book have piqued your curiosity and inspired you to discover additional tools and insights for your journey, read on!

As a purchaser of our book you receive direct access to our Upside Premium Area, located on our website: www.upsidematters.org/premium.

- **Take the Upside Life Assessment.** The Upside Life Assessment is a free and easy-to-use tool designed to help you begin to get a picture of your sense of true personal wealth and worth—and we're not referring to money in the bank. Completing the Upside Life Assessment takes only moments to complete but a lifetime—yours!—to enrich and refine. Let us help you identify your current areas of strength—as well as the aspects of your life that could use some improvement— as you discover your personalized plan of action for obtaining true (real) wealth. You'll also find instructive video clips by co-author Steve Goldberg on the five Upside Life Accounts for measuring true wealth.

- **Begin each week on the Upside.** Join the many others now receiving their Monday morning inspiration via our weekly web column/weblog called *Starting Your Week on the Upside.* Subscription is free! Access our complete archive of posts and sign up to receive your own copy in your inbox every Monday morning. Go to www.upsidematters.org

■ **Find links to other books, websites, articles, videos, and related sources of information and inspiration.** There are countless excellent resources available out there to help you clarify your next steps and light your continuing journey of self-discovery. We have compiled lists of selected resources and further reading and have provided you with links to locate them easily. Please visit our website at: www.upsidematters.org

■ **Share your experience with the authors.** If you're willing to share your comments on the book and/or your own Upside experiences, we'd love to hear from you. Please contact us care of: www.upsidematters.org

■ **Get help in getting started.** If you encounter any problems accessing our Premium Area, or have questions about any of the content, contact support@upsidematters.org

*Best wishes on your journey...*
*Barbara and Steve*

### Please use the following email addresses to contact Barbara and Steve directly:

Barbara Taylor:
barbara@upsidematters.org

Steve Goldberg:
steve@upsidematters.org

# About the Authors

■ **Steve Goldberg** has worked as an executive, career, and personal coach/adviser for the past thirty years. His work has taken him around the globe to more than twenty countries to deliver coaching and organizational effectiveness programs to Fortune 500 corporations, UN organizations, and international gov-  ernmental agencies including AT&T, Accenture, Ford Motor Company, US Postal Service, and World Health Organization.

Steve holds a master's degree in education from Harvard University, where he focused his studies in adult learning and development. He has met and worked with some of the wealthiest people on the planet as well as some of the poorest, which has offered him important insights about life and living it fully.

■ **Barbara A. Taylor** is a Canadian family therapist, writer, art student, wife, and mother of grown daughters who is currently on sabbatical from clinical practice work while living as an expatriate in St. Paul, MN. Barbara served as editor of the weekly web column *Starting Your Week on the Upside* during its initial year. This is her first book.

6956069R0

Made in the USA
Charleston, SC
03 January 2011